GOOD ENOUGH IS
GOOD ENOUGH

"This book shares in the greatness of all books that tell the truth. People who long for depth in our superficial culture will find refreshment here, and people who suspect social media doesn't always tell the whole story will find genuine companionship."

Grace Mazza Urbanski
Author of *Pray with Me*

"Every mother has experienced that awful moment when she discovers that no matter how hard she tries, she will never get it all right; she will never be a perfect parent. With this book, Colleen Duggan has written the sane and sensible way to refine on that impossible goal. Raising children who know they are loved unconditionally and who know who they are and where they fit in really is 'good enough.' In fact, it might be a close to perfection as we will ever get."

Elizabeth Scalia
US editor of *Aleteia* and author of *Strange Gods*

"Colleen Duggan bares herself in an unprecedented way for the betterment of moms everywhere. *Good Enough Is Good Enough* is not just a fabulous read for you but also your best friend and for the mom down the street. This is more than a pat on the back; it's a soothing balm for your soul and a cheery cup of tea for your weary heart. Know, moms, that there is hope for you, for your family, and for eternity. This book will be treasured for the wisdom it contains and for the gem of hope it uncovers for moms everywhere."

Sarah A. Reinhard
Catholic author, blogger, and coeditor of
The Catholic Mom's Prayer Companion

"I am thrilled by Colleen's honesty. Her transparency about the challenges she has faced in her own faith walk invites us into a deeper consideration of our own imperfections."

From the foreword by **Lisa M. Hendey**
Founder of *CatholicMom.com*

"We are grateful for Colleen Duggan's honest, soul-searching reflection on motherhood, which we hope will be a blessing to those who struggle against cultural messages that demand perfection of moms today. Colleen reminds us that God's grace perfects our always-imperfect nature if we are honest with ourselves and God. Thank you, Colleen, for this hope-filled call to all of us who are imperfect parents!"

Tim and Sue Muldoon
Coauthors of *The Discerning Parent*

GOOD ENOUGH IS GOOD ENOUGH

confessions of an imperfect
• catholic mom •

COLLEEN DUGGAN

Foreword by Lisa M. Hendey

AVE MARIA PRESS AVE Notre Dame, Indiana

© 2018 by Colleen Duggan

Founded in 1865, Ave Maria Press is a ministry of the United States Province of Holy Cross.

www.avemariapress.com

Paperback: ISBN-13 978-1-59471-731-4

E-book: ISBN-13 978-1-59471-732-1

Cover image © plainpicture by Charles Gullung.

Cover and text design by Katherine Ann Robinson.

Printed and bound in the United States of America.

Library of Congress Cataloging-in-Publication Data is available.

To My Parents

St. Paul wrote, "And now these three remain: faith, hope and love. But the greatest of these is love." In our family, we always had what was greatest.

To John

In his spiritual autobiography *A Severe Mercy*, Sheldon Vanauken said anything valuable he ever wrote came as a direct result of the marriage of his mind and his spirit with his late wife, Davy. I second his sentiments.

To My Kids

I pray my love for you really will cover my multitude of sins. For all the times I've reacted instead of responded and for the many times I've failed you, I'm sorry. Always remember this: Your worth comes not from what you do but from who you are. I loved you before you were born and I will into eternity.

Now what was the sort of "hole" man had got himself into? He had tried to set up on his own, to behave as if he belonged to himself. In other words, fallen man is not simply an imperfect creature who needs improvement: he is a rebel who must lay down his arms. Laying down your arms, surrendering, saying you are sorry, realizing that you have been on the wrong track and getting ready to start life over again from the ground floor—this is the only way out of our "hole." This process of surrender—this movement full speed astern—is what Christians call repentance. Now repentance is no fun at all. . . . It means unlearning all the self-conceit and self-will that we have been training ourselves into for thousands of years. It means killing part of yourself, undergoing a kind of death.

—C. S. Lewis, *Mere Christianity*

What was not included in my plans lay in God's plan.

—Edith Stein, *Life in a Jewish Family*

CONTENTS

FOREWORD
BY LISA M. HENDEY

I've often considered it a very great blessing that Jesus did not say to his followers, "Come to me all you who totally have your act together, and I will give you rest."

No, nestled instead at the end of Matthew's eleventh chapter are words that have often been a balm to my overwhelmed mother's heart: "Come to me, all you who labor and are burdened, and I will give you rest. Take my yoke upon you and learn from me, for I am meek and humble of heart; and you will find rest for yourselves. For my yoke is easy, and my burden light" (Mt 11:28–30).

If you are the type of mother who regularly excoriates herself for not being "enough" for your husband and children, then the book you are about to read should be as soothing to your soul as those words Jesus spoke to the very imperfect band of disciples he hand selected. Make no mistake: Jesus wasn't teaching early Christians that religion doesn't matter or that we, all these years later, could have a "Get Out of Mass Free" card if we have to share our pew with a petulant toddler each Sunday. Rather, he was unburdening them from the often harsh, detailed law of the scribes and Pharisees. Jesus invited them, and us thousands of years later, into an ever-deepening relationship with him and his Word. When we gather to receive the Eucharist, and especially when we gift our children with the faith, we follow directly in the footsteps of those who were invited into this rest, this lightened yoke, this bearable burden.

But Jesus never said it was going to be easy. And the encouragement shared in the following pages by Colleen Duggan is direct witness to some of the challenges that come with being part of a domestic church. Some of what you will read here will make you wince. Some of it may stir old wounds in your troubled heart. But, personally, I am thrilled by Colleen's honesty. Her transparency about the challenges she has faced in her own faith walk invites us into a deeper consideration of our own imperfections.

I'll save you the drama of laying out too many of my own faults. But those of you who have ventured through our community at CatholicMom.com may know that our apostolate was directly born of my own desperate longing to find some way—any way—to figure out how to *do* this life of being a faithful Catholic mom. Raised in a loving home, I was given the gift of a Catholic upbringing by my parents and nurtured in a parish that made it easy for me to know the unconditional love of our Creator. But while my childhood catechesis (or lack thereof) in those immediate post–Vatican II pews helped me to fall in love with Jesus and his Church, I knew very little about the tangible "stuff" that came along with being a Catholic. What started as my personal quest to know and love my faith so that I could pass it to my two sons has, through the power of the Holy Spirit, become a vibrant community of souls who gather daily to learn to more joyfully live out our vocations.

In each of the women I've met through our community, I've encountered facets of the very challenges I face daily in my own home and parish: the desire to give God and my family my very best while never feeling that I am "enough": good enough, holy enough, serving enough, praying enough. You know the list, because you live this journey too. I recently came across a passage on prayer written by Servant of God Catherine Doherty, herself a Catholic mom:

> All of this can only come about through prayer, and the greatest prayer is the Eucharist. Times spent before the Blessed Sacrament and in chapel form part of this prayer. Of course, prayer is much broader than all these. Prayer is as infinite as God. Prayer is constant. Prayer is work. Prayer is loving. Prayer is dying. Prayer is stripping oneself of one's needs. Prayer is serving the needs of others. Prayer is conversation with God that never ceases. Prayer is life in Nazareth, and doing the work of Our Lady, or working with St. Joseph in the carpentry shop. Prayer is living in the presence of God.[1]

Catherine Doherty recognized that in our own homes we can emulate the love of those hidden years of Mary in Nazareth—the ones filled with a toddler and laundry and chores and all played out far from helpful family. And while we never want to neglect our devotion to the sacraments, it's time for those of us who never feel "good enough" to seek solace in those moments of the day when Jesus is with us, right where we are and just as we are. Let's fold ourselves into his loving arms the next time we feel everything swirling out of control. Never forget that you are God's beautiful daughter, wonderfully made for this exact moment in time. With, in, and through him, you are always enough.

ACKNOWLEDGMENTS

People often comment that it takes a village to raise a child, and while this is consistent with my parenting experience, it's also consistent with my book-writing experience. The following people were instrumental in making this work possible:

To Randy Hain, my editor at Integrated Catholic Life, thank you for taking me under your wing and encouraging me to tell my story. I will be forever grateful for our introduction and our many good years of work together.

To Rhonda Ortiz, my graphic design ninja and most trusted writing companion, thank you for the countless hours you've spent reading, editing, and redesigning my work. You will never know how much I value your input, prayers, and assistance both in life and in writing.

To Cristina Trinidad, who knows all things about social media and promotion, thank you for your help, your dedication, and your encouragement to plug away for at least fifteen minutes a day, which is good advice for all hard things, really.

To Jeannie Hannaman, Alexis Love, Crystal Edwards, and Karen Landry, thank you for your invaluable reading of the first drafts of this manuscript. Handing over a working manuscript is akin to asking for constructive parenting advice on how to raise your firstborn child. It's tricky business, but I couldn't have asked for more helpful people to offer gentle, honest feedback.

To Amber Elder, for your kindness, conscientious-ness, vision, and your on-point suggestions. I've loved working with you.

To my mom and dad: I'm indebted to you for your help with the kids so I could work and write and write and work.

To John, for the hundreds of bowls of cereal you poured and all the sack lunches you prepared without complaint and without being asked so I could write this book, thank you.

And to my kids: you are the biggest squad of cheer-leaders ever. Thanks for believing I could do it.

INTRODUCTION

I've always been bad. Probably I shall be bad again,
punished again. But the worse I am, the more I need
God. I can't shut myself out from His mercy.
—Evelyn Waugh, *Brideshead Revisited*

I grew up the oldest child in an alcoholic home. My
father, to whom I jokingly refer as "The Colonel" because
of his rank in the Marine Corps, is a Vietnam War vet-
eran, and his experiences during war chased after him
with as much tenacity as a tiger hunts its prey. The Colonel was willing to lay down his life for his country, and
his decision to serve was one that had consequences. He
walked into war, and when he left he was permanently
altered. War takes more than just casualties, and, for a
long time, it took my dad in the form of booze.

The Colonel is a person of deep integrity. He's the
type of guy who buys three tickets to get into the movie
theatre but when he accidentally receives four, goes back
to return or pay for the extra. He excelled as an attack
pilot, climbing the ranks in the Marine Corps and retir-
ing as a colonel shortly after Bill Clinton was elected
president.

Last year, I asked him what he was reading, and he
brought me a mound of books piled several feet in the
air. Most of the titles were on history and war, and he
excitedly shared little snippets from each one. For more
than twenty minutes, he gave an oral report on George
Washington, filled with random but interesting pieces of
information all about Washington's life and worldview.

Maybe it's because he reads so much, but the Colonel is also a great storyteller. In fact, I like to think my ability to spin a tale comes from him, and he's read everything I've written and always encouraged me to write a book. He stayed with us recently for a few weeks while my parents waited for their new house to become available, and my husband, John, marveled on more than one occasion about the amazing life my dad has led and the great joie de vivre with which he relays an anecdote.

As a child, my father was an altar boy and attended Catholic schools and university. After Vietnam, he went in and out of the Church for a while but eventually found his way back. Now he never misses Sunday Mass. Still, his alcoholism affected our lives, especially when I was a kid. My mother once told me that when they were newly married, my dad had a nightmare that caused him to thrash around in the bed and awaken her. She reached over to shake him out of his slumber, but she startled him instead. My dad sprung on top of her, held her down, and then darted under the bed. When my father realized what happened, he crawled out, sheepish and remorseful. He felt terrible for his reaction, but before they went back to bed he warned her never to touch him again while he was asleep.

These were the demons my father brought into marriage, and he tried to put the squeeze on them with alcohol. As an abuse survivor, my mother had her own demons, which plagued her and from which she sought comfort in food and caretaking. Her personal sufferings haunted her just as my dad's haunted him, and many of those early years of their marriage and parenting were spent trying to survive life amid the emotional pain they brought with them into marriage. As a consequence, the way in which they related to each other and to their children was often distorted.

My Modus Operandi

As the oldest child, I became a high performer to distract attention away from the addiction in our household. I felt responsible for the negative things happening around me, so I put on a positive public face at home, even though it felt like our home life was crumbling from the inside. I threw myself into all things academic. I was an honors student. I was involved in as many extracurricular activities as possible. I protected and took care of my siblings. I tolerated friends who were self-absorbed and used me because it was easier to accept poor friendships than to accept the loneliness I sometimes experienced at home. I never got in trouble. I did all I could to succeed in order to hide any appearance of my family's dysfunction.

When I graduated high school, I first went to Saint Mary's College to study religion and psychology and afterward was accepted into a teaching program at the University of Notre Dame on full scholarship. While at these schools, I carried my overachieving tendencies with me and threw myself into making straight A's. In my first real job as a teacher I worked eighty hours a week, creating well-planned lessons and volunteering as the coach and moderator for several sports and clubs. I took up exercise and skipped meals in order to stay thin. By the time I met John, my need to do everything The Right Way was no longer about bringing honor to my family; this was how I lived in the world. When I married, I carried all these tendencies with me and applied my intense approach to life to my roles as a wife, mother, and Catholic. I was desperate to be a good spouse and parent who produced good, Catholic children in a dysfunction-free home, and I set to work trying to figure out the best way to make that happen. I joined Bible studies, I read papal encyclicals, I pored over all the Catholic parenting books, and I consulted women I admired for advice on raising Catholic kids. I took Natural Family Planning classes, attended daily Mass, made regular Confession, sought spiritual direction, and went to Catholic conventions. I studied the Church's teachings, read about the lives of the saints, and talked with priests about Catholic family life. My ideals and my research coupled with my intense approach to life helped cultivate romantic, unrealistic notions about what our Catholic family life should look like.

I loved Jesus and wanted to follow him. I was devoted to the Catholic Church and the truths she contained, and I was committed to raising Catholic kids, but several things worked against me. I didn't realize how much my quest for The Perfect Catholic Family was motivated by the desire to correct certain broken aspects of my own childhood. I also thought my Catholic faith would be a sort of insurance policy I bought to protect myself and my children from sin and suffering. If we followed Jesus and the Church's teachings, we reduced, at least in my mind, the potential risks we might face in life: illness, adultery, more addiction, financial ruin, and other pains.

The coping mechanisms that helped me to operate in my family of origin, that had helped me while I was growing up in an alcoholic home, eventually caused problems with the family my husband and I were making. I felt a high burden of responsibility to meet the needs of others, even if it meant neglecting myself.[1] I also had trouble accepting my humanity because it meant embracing both my personal strengths *and* weaknesses as a wife and mother. (And I hated my weaknesses, wished them away, and white-knuckled through self-improvement plans to get rid of them.) I erroneously believed good eating, sleeping, and exercising were for the weak and self-absorbed, so I disregarded my need for any type of basic self-care. It was difficult for me to honestly express certain wants, desires, and needs, so the way I related to John and my kids was immature and inauthentic. I had ridiculous, unrealistic expectations of myself, but also of John and my children. Why should I have to explain to John what I needed to feel loved and secure? Shouldn't he know? (Alas, he didn't know, and I did have to explain it, I soon figured out.) I struggled to understand and accept normal, typical behavior for children because what I thought they were capable of emotionally, physically, mentally, and spiritually was not consistent with what they were actually truly capable of emotionally, physically, mentally, and spiritually. Despite my commitment to be a good wife and mother and to live in a way that would get all of us into heaven, I cultivated some pretty toxic notions about how to make it happen.

I embraced an entire set of unconscious ideas about Catholic parenting that were based on lies. Looking back, these lies seem so obvious and so blatant it might be hard for a faithful Christian to understand how I developed them in the first place. The thing is, intellectually I understood God was supposed to be the ruler of my life, but my actions didn't reflect that "conviction." My behavior conveyed a subconscious belief it was up to *me* to become a saint and to make sure my entire family became saints too. This crack in my intellectual foundation happened when I was a child, when

I thought I was to blame for all the tragedies in life. I carried this idea with me into adulthood and tried my very best to protect everyone I loved from pain and suffering. I controlled people and situations, and I adopted ideas about Catholic parenting I thought would keep us safe. I thought, for instance, it was up to me to get everything right, or else I would destroy my kids' lives. I thought I had to sacrifice everything—including my very self—for my children. I believed I needed to create perfect little Catholics (even though I had no clue as to how to accomplish that lofty goal; I couldn't even teach my toddler how to make the correct Sign of the Cross!) and that if I exposed my kids to the Catholic faith, they would love and eventually adopt the faith for their own. When I looked around at the families sitting next to me in the pews on Sunday, I was convinced that they had mastered that secret Catholic family life code that made everything fall into place, and I couldn't. Their ability to implement certain parenting practices guaranteed, in my mind, faithful adult children, while my own failure to implement certain best practices would be cause for our family's tragic end.

In the end, my Catholic faith unearthed these harmful ideas I embraced about parenting and family life. When I entered into marriage and motherhood, I thought if I just worked hard enough, applied enough effort, and perfected myself and my family enough, we would become a family of Catholic saints. The problem was, nothing I did ever worked. I was the exact opposite of the kind of perfection I envisioned. While I might have wanted to consistently respond lovingly to John and my kids, my sinfulness, past wounds, imperfections, and frenetic lifestyle made that a really difficult goal. For so long, I tried to keep it all together and do everything right, which made life stressful and more difficult. It strained my marriage and left me an angry, impatient wife and mother instead of the loving, joyful wife and mother I longed to be. The reality of my life was far from what I craved. I fell flat on my face, and it was messy. While I lay there, crying and defeated, I begged for God's help. I crawled into the confessional and laid my sins before the priest. I dragged myself down the aisle to Communion and implored God to heal me. I slouched in a chair in a priest or a therapist's office and poured out my wounded heart.

God used these experiences and people to guide and heal me. He came to my rescue not because I was holy and successful and perfect but because I wasn't any of those things. He offered his aid because I was weak; I needed him and could do no actual good without him. Though I set out to win at Catholic parenting and family life, my rubric didn't work. I failed. I floundered. I sinned. I came face-to-face with my human weaknesses and those of my family members.

In 2 Corinthians 12:9, St. Paul writes, "he said to me, 'My grace is sufficient for you, for power is made perfect in weakness.'" As I came face-to-face with my limited humanity, God infused his power into all my mess-ups, and his grace exposed the cracks in my thinking. He uncovered the poisonous notions about my Catholic family, notions I held so dear, and he put me on a different path—not a path of control and perfection but a path of surrendering to his will perfectly, which is quite a different thing indeed.

As it turns out, what God actually wanted from me and for me was a lot different than what I thought. In some ways, his call to relinquish my ideas about Catholic family life was costlier than what I had demanded of myself, because it required an acceptance of myself as I was: imperfect and weak, a woman without a cape and often barely able to get out of bed in the mornings. It meant accepting my limitations, not ignoring them and powering through. It meant accepting my family members for who they are and how God made them, not wishing they were wired a different way. It meant accepting suffering and pain and heartache and difficulty but finding tremendous freedom and peace even in the midst of all of those things. It meant no longer comparing my failures and successes to those around me but offering empathy and kindness to the people I encountered who were also struggling.

The book you are holding in your hand is the revelation of part of my journey. Make no mistake: this is not a didactic treatise on how to overcome controlling, perfectionistic tendencies. I can't write that book while my own recovery is still unfolding. Rather, these words are the result of my own broken journey toward sanctity, not in the way *I* wanted but in the way God wants for me. I'm not totally healed of my intense inclinations, but I have grown.

I now root my identity not in being a perfect Catholic with the perfect Catholic family but in who I am in Jesus Christ. I have experienced relief from the compulsive desire to do all and be all things to all people. I don't covet what is impossible anymore but accept what is—a family that is most definitely not perfect but is mine. The book you are holding in your hand shares the process of how some of that healing happened.

This book examines some of the flawed notions I embraced about Catholic parenting and how I came to believe them in the first place. I share the experiences and the encounters with people who helped me identify how these ideas poisoned my life and my relationships. Sprinkled throughout are personal stories, scripture passages, examples from the lives of the saints, and various quotations from the *Catechism of the Catholic Church*. At the end of each chapter, you will find a closing prayer and reflection.

Maybe you didn't grow up in a home with addiction, but maybe somewhere along the line you started to believe some of the same lies I did about Catholic family life. Maybe you feel like everything is up to you, that you have to get everything right or you'll destroy your kids' lives. Maybe you think creating perfect Catholics who stay Catholic is something you can control. Maybe you struggle with doing everything "right" but know the ill effect of this approach to life. If so, this book if for you.

I pray it helps.

Confession 1

I DON'T KNOW HOW TO MASTER MOTHERHOOD

> If you live in the dark a long time and the sun comes out, you do not cross into it whistling. There's an initial uprush of relief at first, then—for me, anyway—a profound dislocation. My old assumptions about how the world works are buried, yet my new ones aren't yet operational. There's been a death of sorts, but without a few days in hell, no resurrection is possible.
>
> —Mary Karr, *Lit*

My first child, Patrick, was born eleven months after John and I married, and our second, Meaghan, was born just eleven months after Patrick. We had a third baby, Mary, less than two years later. By the time our eighth anniversary rolled around, two more babies had joined our family, Christopher and then Camille, for a grand total of five babies under the age of seven. Our sixth and last baby, Edward, was born one month before our eleventh anniversary.

Almost as soon as I became pregnant with my oldest, I quit my job as a high school religion teacher in order to be a full-time, stay-at-home mother. The switch from the life of a full-time teacher to a full-time wife and mother was hard. Before, I had managed classrooms of at least thirty kids and delegated responsibilities in afterschool clubs, and now I changed diapers and fed babies. Before, I had attended meetings and strategized plans for student success, and now I meal-planned and folded laundry. Before, I had run clubs, sports teams, and classrooms, and now I lived a private life with my small children and daily chores. Who was I, now that I wasn't contributing something valuable and tangible to the workforce? What grand accomplishments did I have to share after a long day of child-wrangling and disciplining? When my husband came home, my reports included updates about organizing the pantry and keeping the toddlers out of the street (which is a heroic task, depending on the kid—let's be honest). As difficult as that work was, I struggled to see the value of my role as an at-home mother in the same way I was able to see the value of my work at the school. To make matters worse, I possessed a deep, unarticulated fear that I was going to be lousy at this whole motherhood gig. At work, I could measure success, monitor accolades, and excel at the tasks I was given, assuming I put in the hard work and effort.

Mastering motherhood was a complete mystery to me.

I wanted to be a perfect parent, a model of mothering, but how did I make that dream a reality? I loved my posse of little people but struggled with the demanding nature of parenting them. Their care and feeding day in and day out was exhausting, and their constant demands forced me to face my weaknesses. While I never would have described myself as selfish before I had kids, I couldn't deny that fact after. A ticker tape of script ran through my brain all day, reflections on the frustrating conundrums I faced as a parent to many little people:

- *Can't you just leave me alone while I pee in peace?*
- *Who cares if the pretzel stick is broken? It still tastes the same!*
- *For the love of all things good and holy, please don't put beads up your sister's nose!*

I was never the poster woman for serenity before I had children, yet the perpetual squabbles among my children, combined with their many demands, exacerbated my impatience. I was both shocked and humbled at how easy it was to feel anger at a small child who had little to no self-control. Parenting challenged me in a way nothing else had. I couldn't escape my imperfections even when I wanted to. Those weaknesses were there before my eyes—and the eyes of my children—all day long.

Another aspect of mothering that challenged me, in a way I could not have foreseen prior to becoming a parent, was all the pressure to make the *right* decisions for my children. From the moment they were born I had to have thoughts and opinions about what would be best for my babies. As soon as the nurse placed Patrick into my arms, I needed to know whether he would take a pacifier, breast or bottle feed, or use cloth or disposable diapers. There were so many decisions it was mindboggling. Moms want to be informed and do what is best for their children, but for me, the need to have a plan about the smallest of details produced overwhelming waves of anxiety.

Like all new parents, I was vulnerable because I didn't have any parenting perspective. I didn't know what I thought about pacifiers (now I know they are latex lifesavers) or disposable diapers (thank goodness for the genius who thought them up) or what would work best for my individual children, so I was quite susceptible to all the latest fads, opinions, and expert advice. The books and the blogs held the truth to everlasting Catholic parenting life—or at the very least offered me tips for getting my kid to quit wetting the bed. Since I wanted to do everything right in my job as a parent, I often sought advice when I should have trusted my instinct. Worse yet, I felt like a complete failure when, for whatever reason, I couldn't follow the suggestions of experts.

It didn't take much for me to feel like a failure, especially if all my friends were able to practice a parenting method I desired but couldn't implement. For instance, every Friday for many years, I participated in a playgroup with some of my closest mom friends and their small children. Each week we'd meet for coffee and donuts, pray the Rosary, and then share parenting strategies, prayers, and support. We had all read a book together on attachment-parenting practices; the book recommended an immediate responsiveness to an infant's needs and continual physical touch between parent and child for most of the day. The author proposed nursing an infant on demand and co-sleeping as a surefire method to ensure proper bonding between baby and mom. Most of us believed this was *the* Catholic way to parent, and we were eager to put the techniques from the book into practice.

The problem was that, unlike the other moms in the playgroup, I had two small babies who were eleven months apart, which made it almost impossible for me to wear both children simultaneously. It was also difficult for me to wear one of them at a time because, if I did, I had trouble bending down to tend to the needs of the other child, or the child who wasn't strapped to me would wail because they weren't being held.

As far as co-sleeping was concerned, I couldn't wrap my head around that logistical nightmare. Imagine what our bed would have looked like if we co-slept with our infant and our eleventh month old! Who would sleep? The children perhaps, and maybe John, but certainly not me. In order to survive and be somewhat coherent during the day, everyone needed to be well rested in order to function to the best of our abilities. Once my babies were old enough to refrain from eating all night long, I trained them to sleep through the night. My decision to do so, one made considering the best interests of everyone in my family, produced anxiety and guilt, particularly when I heard other moms talk about what they were doing. In my circles, we all agreed that the "appropriate" way to parent, the one best for the mother and child, was to co-sleep and nurse on demand. However, given the nature of my life with two babies under a year, I couldn't justify that approach. It didn't work for us. Yet I still felt like a complete failure, even though my children's needs *were* being met and we were all catching enough shuteye, at least most of the time.

On top of feeling like a failure when I couldn't adopt "best" parenting practices, I was harsh with myself for things outside my control. The way I silently spoke to myself throughout the day dripped with a relentless critique of my performance; I wouldn't talk to my worst enemy the way I talked to myself. I remember once after a morning of excursions with my two oldest, just toddlers at the time, we came home and the kids were in meltdown mode because they were hungry and tried. I felt terrible for them. Amid their wailing and gnashing of teeth, I frantically pulled out cheese, meat, crackers, and fruit and put them on little plates for the kids. The entire time I worked I internally critiqued my poor use of time and my inability to tend to my children's needs well.

I filled most of my days with silent commentary on my parenting performance and rarely, if ever, did I make the grade. The errands we ran on the morning my kids had the meltdown were not superfluous. I took the children grocery shopping, and while we were gone the kids became overtired and hungry. It happens when dealing with small children. Yet I blamed myself and believed their emotional states were a direct result of my poor parenting.

Shortly after the morning of toddler meltdowns, I attended spiritual direction with a priest friend. Through tears, I relayed all the ways I was "failing" as a mom. When I finished my litany, Father looked at me, puzzled, and said, "Colleen, did you think you were going to be a perfect parent?"

It was a rhetorical question, so I didn't have the chance to answer out loud, but silently I screamed, *Yes!* Father could see, after just five minutes of talking with me, that I had set completely unrealistic standards for myself.

But I couldn't see it yet.

Failure wasn't an option to me. I had too much at stake—my pride and ego, for starters, but also the lives of my children. I refused to repeat the generational sin of the past, and it was my job to eradicate that blemish from our family history. A laissez-faire approach to parenting wasn't going to work. It was get it all right *or else.*

My constant evaluation of my failure to make the parenting grade kept me joyless and frustrated. By the time I had my fourth baby, I became easily angered over random, irrational things and often lashed out at John, our children, or the clerk at the grocery store. Once I calmed down, I had trouble articulating why I was upset in the first place. John and I would have a fight, and, since neither of us had the tools to communicate effectively, we'd walk around the house in stone cold silence for days or even weeks until one of us apologized. I would lose my patience with one of the kids because they did something normal and kid-like, but the fact I lost my patience at all was so devastating to me I couldn't forgive myself. I would berate myself for my perceived failures—my messy house, my ill-behaved children, my tense marriage—all day, every day. I was overly involved in service work, which did little to renew me personally and left me feeling drained. I was stuck in a series of unhealthy friendships where others didn't know the real me. I listened to the struggles of everyone else—their marital issues and time management and parenting problems—while my own life was falling apart.

I drove myself to keep a perfect house, be a perfect Catholic, look perfect, and maintain perfect familial relationships, and it was all a lie. Nothing was perfect, least of all me. The ruse all came crashing down one day in a moment so profound it would shift and ultimately begin to heal my crippling compulsiveness.

Face-to-Face with Parenting Failures

I was spending an afternoon right after my fourth child was born catching up on laundry, bills, cleaning, and cooking, while my two older children, Patrick and Meaghan, were at school, when the phone rang. My instinct told me to ignore it. I answered anyway and for the next

forty-five minutes was bombarded with a list of responsibilities and to-do items for a volunteer church ministry.

As I "chatted" with the caller, I watched my three-
year-old, Mary Bernadette, unearth a container of small
8,500 multi-colored plastic fuse beads clearly marked
"Not for children age three or younger," climb onto the
kitchen table, and get to work. When she began using
the beads and corresponding pegboards to make a cat,
I thought she could handle the project. However, Mary
Bernadette quickly tired of the tedious bead pegging
activity because, really, placing food grade plastic onto
animal shaped boards is only *just* so fun.

She got more creative.

She stuck her chubby hand deep into the bead
bucket and brought out a fistful of beads. I could see
the wheels in her little toddler brain working overtime.
Hmmm, she wondered, *what will happen if I do this?*

She stood up on the kitchen table and slowly
opened her hand, watching those beads fall away like
sand through a sieve. The beads bounced off the table;
a rainbow of red, green, blue, orange, and purple show-
ered the floor. They flew under the couch and into the
crevices of my floorboards. Everywhere I looked was
covered with multi-colored plastic.

This new experiment delighted her and her desire
for greater bead-tossing creativity grew. Again she dug
deep in the bucket and this time when she came up, both
hands were filled with beads, which she again dutifully
dropped onto the floor and table. I tried to get off the
phone, but the caller kept speaking, and because I didn't
want to be rude, I made a catastrophic decision—I didn't
hang up. This story ends with Mary Bernadette, in complete and utter toddler delight, hurling the entire bucket
filled with 8,500 beads into the air. The beads flew in

every direction and left me with a hot, multi-colored, plastic mess.

All parents sometimes lose patience with their children. It happens to the best of us. But the way I reacted to Mary Bernadette after I finally got off the phone wasn't just a weak moment. I felt out of control, capable of hurting her, and it scared me. Despite my actions, I wasn't angry that Mary Bernadette had spilled 8,500 beads all over the floor, or even at my new to-do list for our parish. I was actually angry about a whole host of unresolved issues that kept bubbling to the surface while I kept trying to push them down.

The first step in the Twelve Step program as outlined in Alcoholics Anonymous states, "We admitted we were powerless over alcohol—that our lives had become unmanageable."[1] While I wasn't an alcoholic, I knew alcohol was still very much affecting my life. In that moment, it was obvious my life had become unmanageable. I loved my husband and children very much, but I recognized it wasn't enough for me to love them. I needed healing from past wounds stemming from my dad's alcoholism, and I needed to examine the wicked streak of perfectionism I possessed, which motivated me to attack life with such intensity. I needed to know how to manage my emotions better so I wouldn't flip out when my children threw buckets of beads all over the place. I needed to know how to respond to my family members as individuals and give them what they needed—including boundaries, time, attention, and personal space. I needed to develop a different set of relational skills with John, especially when it came to resolving marital issues. In short, I had to learn how to manage myself and quit trying to manage everyone else.

That afternoon, I picked up the phone and called a counselor. I knew it was time to examine what was at the root of this incident and of my other struggles as a wife and mother, so I could be better for my family. I didn't have the proper emotional tools to deal with life, and I knew I needed someone to help me develop the right ones, so I called a Catholic therapist and began to see him regularly.

In the years that followed, I sought counsel from this person who educated and directed me on the right course of action—right given my personal history, temperament, and life situation. Piece by piece we talked about the elements of my life that weren't working— my marital issues, parenting struggles, and relationship challenges—and then we outlined avenues to change. Then I implemented those changes as best I could. Counseling helped me to begin to let go of the notion that I had to do everything right or doom all of us to failure. I started to understand sometimes a good enough approach rather than a perfect one was just that: good enough. The emotional work necessary in counseling was hard, but it put me on the path to healing and freedom.

Accepting Myself as I Am

When I first arrived at his office, my counselor asked me a series of questions to assess how he could best help me. Throughout our work together, I noticed his questions always prompted self-reflection, which helped me know myself in new ways. I felt desperate, distraught at my unpredictable sweeps of emotions, so I didn't hold back when he gently probed me about why I reacted to certain people or situations in the ways I did. I didn't want to lose my temper so easily, and I figured it couldn't hurt to be honest with him. He was, after all, trained to help.

I told him about what happened with Mary Bernadette and the beads, how I wanted to be a good parent but had difficulty expressing emotion appropriately. I told him about my fear of losing control, which meant I walked around with a tight grip on life, anxious and fearful that if I surrendered, everything would fall apart. I told him about how I ignored my own wants, needs, and feelings in favor of serving others.

Over the course of our meetings, we examined how my strengths and weaknesses were at work in different types of situations. He helped me see how certain people, relationships, or activities triggered my tendency to want to "save" people or do things for others they should do for themselves, and he encouraged me to pay attention to how I felt. Tuning in to my own emotional responses was a novel concept to me, since I chronically regarded my own emotions as inconsequential. Becoming aware of myself was life altering, because I started to recognize some of the reasons I was so easily angered. For instance, I felt guilty and stressed all the time about my failure to parent a certain way, even when that way didn't appeal to the strengths of my temperament and those of my children. No wonder I snapped at the kids or John so easily! Despite the fact that I was all in as a mother, that I devoted my entire self to my family, I could only see what I wasn't doing. Through counseling, I realized it was better to use common sense and implement methods that worked for me given my situation, resources, and personality than to try to force solutions that didn't work for me or my kids.

Another thing my counselor helped me recognize was that there were too many drains on my time and energy. I felt as if my sanity might snap at any moment, because I had allowed outside responsibilities and relationships to impose on and take over my life. To rectify my frayed and frazzled state and to help me regain a sense of emotional equilibrium, I was gently encouraged to back out of any extra commitments and to go back to the basics—to focus on my family and me, which was a full time job in and of itself. My counselor reminded me many times that being a full time mother to four children was an overwhelming, exhausting, important job, and that I needed to be gentle with myself rather than harsh and overly demanding.

And as it turned out, I wasn't all weak and broken as I had feared. Therapy helped me to see the good things about myself, not just the bad ones. I loved my family very much and was devoted to them. I was a passionate person, and this passion allowed me to freely live my faith and articulate my love and affection for those around me, not always perfectly, but consistently. I was organized and energetic, prone to anger, yes, but I had a zeal for life and a genuine interest in other people. As it turns out, the energy I had at work for my school and my students translated easily into the care I poured into my home and my family. I realized I was a leader, with the God-given ability to multitask and command various projects all at once. I had weaknesses I needed to pray for the grace to overcome, but those weaknesses did not have to define and ruin me. My whole life's purpose didn't need to be focused on eliminating my self-perceived "badness" from my very being.

I didn't need to wish I had been born a different way or to force my sometimes-volatile nature into an unrealistic vapid serenity. Beating myself up for all my inadequacies was a waste of time. I could accept myself as God made me—weaknesses included—and then I needed to turn to him to make me well. I slowly learned to trust that the Lord *would* heal me, but that it would be in his good time and in his good way. I abandoned the notion that it was my job to rip my weaknesses up from their very roots and instead trusted God with the uprooting. Even the way I spoke to God required conversion; I needed to abandon the frantic, worried, compulsive sermons I was inclined to issue in prayer in favor of more gentle requests to God about what it was *he* wanted from and for me. God's way required me to let go of my own white-knuckled efforts to change and instead offer my trust and surrender to him.

In his brilliant treatise on spiritual freedom, Fr. Jacques Philippe writes:

> A great deal of time can be wasted in the spiritual life complaining that we are not like this or not like that, lamenting this defect or that limitation, imagining all the good we could do if, instead of being the way we are, we were less defective, more gifted with this or that quality or virtue, and so on. Here is a waste of time and energy that merely impedes the work of the Holy Spirit in our hearts.
>
> What often blocks the action of God's grace in our lives is less our sins or failings, than it is our failure to accept our own weakness—all those rejections, conscious or not, of what we really are or of our real situation. To "set grace free" in our lives, and paving the way for deep and spectacular changes, it sometimes would be enough to say simply "yes"—a "yes" inspired by trust in God to aspects of our lives we've been rejecting. We refuse to admit that we have this defect, that weak point, were marked by this event, fell into that sin. And so we block the Holy Spirit's action, since he can only

affect our reality to the extent that we accept ourselves. The Holy Spirit never acts unless we freely
cooperate. We must accept ourselves just as we are,
if the Holy Spirit is to change us for better.[2]

One of the most important lessons I learned in my
counselor's office is that I must accept myself as I am, a
person imbued with both positive and negative traits.
My weaknesses are aspects of who I am; they are part
of me, but they do no not define me as a whole. Counseling allowed me to see it was possible to live with two
incongruous things; I didn't have to hate myself because
I wasn't perfect. It was possible to accept and live with
both the good and the not-so-good things about me.

Self-acceptance didn't require I abdicate attempts
to get better; I simply needed to adapt my approach.
Self-acceptance also meant acknowledging I wouldn't
get it all right and it was impossible to know with 100
percent certainty the correct course of action for my
family all the time (though I could trust God to always
guide me). I needed to surrender, to acknowledge I
would sometimes mess up with John and my kids. I
didn't need to be surprised or aghast when it happened.
I needed to ask for God's forgiveness, rectify the situation with my family, and resolve to do better next time.
Most importantly, I needed to accept that it wasn't my
job to make all things well, but I could have confidence
in God to make good out of anything, even my broken
parenting. My brokenness, in fact, prevents perfection,
and that's OK.

God is still in charge, even when I've messed up.

Accepting Life's Messiness

My own self-acceptance made it a lot easier to accept the
people around me. Instead of shaming them for their

natural inclinations or wishing they were wired a different way, I recognized God gave my husband and kids their own strengths and weaknesses that are different from my own. My children are not miniature carbon copies of John and me. They are their own people, on their own spiritual journeys. The lessons they have to learn are different than mine. I can help them down their paths, but I don't have to feel overly responsible for whether they get it right away. I also don't have to claim responsibility for their weaknesses. Perhaps my child has a bad temper because he sometimes has seen bad example, but perhaps God has allowed that cross to aid my child in his own holiness. My children are their own people, and, while I'm responsible for guiding them, I don't have to blame myself for all their negative tendencies. I never want to neglect my important role in forming their consciences and orienting them toward the good, but I don't need to assume I'm the reason they have particular flaws.

I also started to accept and recognize certain undesirable life situations and the cantankerous moods of those I love as part of the human condition. Interacting with family members, especially when you live with several other people, can be challenging and inconvenient. Accepting that fact is a lot easier and leads me to use greater patience and kindness than trying to control situations or people or fight against reality. Instead of expecting my children to be patient, kind, and loving, I have to be those things, even when my children can't or won't return the gesture. I still have to act like a grown up even when it feels like my kids are doing everything they can to make me miserable.

And though I love them with my entire being, my children *are* sometimes difficult.

A few years ago, John organized a family trip to ven-
erate the traveling body of St. Maria Goretti. I wanted
to enjoy our evening out together, so before we left, I
assisted my preteen with her homework. Pre-adoles-
cence has been hard for her; until recently, I swore she
was quite possibly the easiest child to ever exist on the
planet. On this day, though, she was tired and overwhelmed, which resulted in an epic meltdown consist-
ing of ripped homework, wailing, and slammed doors.

After an hour-long drama fest, I realized no logical
discussion would alleviate her emotional tirade, and I
had the idea to offer her a hug. It was then my sweet
daughter, with heaving sobs, ran into my arms and
had a good cry. As she wept, my heart, just a moment
before hardened and detached, softened. I was moved
with pity for her. The embrace set our interaction on the
right track again. The entire time she had her tantrum I
prayed for a way to overcome my natural desire to inflict
punishment on this struggling child. God answered my
prayer in a moment of grace when he let me know what
she needed was empathy, love, and reassurance (the
very last things I wanted to offer her, by the way). That's
partly what makes this whole parenting gig hard: we
are always struggling with the weight of our own brokenness while our children struggle with the weight of
theirs. It's exhausting.

Accepting life and our family members as they are
isn't always easy. In fact, some of the greatest saints in
the history of the Catholic Church had to put up with
difficult people. One such person was St. Thérèse of
Lisieux, who writes about the rudeness she experienced
at the hands of another religious sister in the convent in
which she lived. In her spiritual memoir, *Story of a Soul*,
St. Thérèse relays this story:

There is in the Community a Sister who has the faculty of displeasing me in everything, in her ways, her words, her character, everything seems very disagreeable to me. . . . Not wishing to give into to the natural antipathy I was experiencing, I told myself that charity must not consist in feelings but in works; then I set myself to doing for this Sister what I would do for the person I loved most. Each time I met her I prayed to God for her, offering him all her virtues and merits. . . . I wasn't content simply with praying very much for this Sister who gave me so many struggles, but I took care to render her all the services possible, and when I was tempted to answer her back in a disagreeable manner, I was content with giving her my most friendly smile, and with changing the subject of the conversation. . . .

As she was absolutely unaware of my feelings for her, never did she suspect the motive for my conduct and she remained convinced that her character was very pleasing to me. One day at recreation she asked in almost these words: "Would you tell me, Sister Thérèse of the Child Jesus, what attracts you so much toward me; every time you look at me, I see you smile?" Ah what attracted me was Jesus hidden in the depths of her soul; Jesus who makes sweet what is most bitter.[3]

Clearly, Thérèse knew what it was like to exist among challenging souls, and she was honest about her natural distaste for another sister in the cloister. She knew it was wrong to nurture those dislikes, so she did all in her power to correct them, but she didn't deny her ill feelings for the woman.

It's tempting for me to want to brush off Thérèse's saintly example. Her way of existing in the world is completely different than mine, and her personal writings are so saccharine, I have to combat my tendency to disregard her experience as inapplicable to my life as a parent of six in modern-day America. Thérèse was an unmarried Carmelite nun living a cloistered life far from the everyday world. In her short life, she was never haggard from long nights pacing floors with a sick baby. She didn't know the volatile nature of a fight with a spouse. She wasn't confronted with the challenge of changing explosive dirty diaper after explosive dirty diaper while managing squabbles between children. She received the sacraments daily and spent many hours in quiet prayer, both of which are electrical conduits for God's grace. Thérèse also had a group of people with whom to share the workload; she wasn't solely responsible for cooking, cleaning, and paying the convent bills. She always had a bed and food to eat, even if it wasn't her favorite entrée, and she never had to worry about money. Sure, she lived with a bunch of women, but exactly how hard was *that*?

Just because Thérèse lived in a convent didn't mean the women she lived with were holy. They were on some occasions bad tempered and annoying. For instance, at chapel Thérèse sat in front of a sister who unintentionally made a clicking noise with her rosary. The noise irritated Thérèse to such a degree she had to will herself not to turn around and glare at the inconsiderate woman. Thérèse also took it upon herself to usher a cranky nun to dinner each evening, though the older woman complained about Thérèse *to* Thérèse the entire time.[4] These anecdotes from the pen of this great saint remind me that part of the journey to holiness requires we learn not only to put up with ourselves but also to put up with others and the imperfect scenarios we sometimes find ourselves in. When we live in community—whether it is in the convent or in a family—someone *will* do something we find irksome or distasteful (and sometimes that person is us). Existing with others is part of life, which is why I find Thérèse's "little way"—doing all things, even small ones, for God—helpful when it comes to accepting life's messiness. The little way reminds me I have two choices: I can scream and kick and fuss because my family members and I sometimes behave in a repulsive and an inconvenient manner, or I can see these inconveniences as opportunities willed by God for a greater purpose, namely my sanctification and the sanctification of my family members.

In one of my favorite spiritual works of all time, *I Believe in Love*, Fr. Jean C. J. d'Elbee puts it like this:

> Remember that each event in your life brings you Jesus' will, which is Jesus Himself. It is he whom you can embrace in everything that comes to you. I bless Him, therefore, however my nature may protest. It will protest. There will be interior seething; there will revolt of the senses; there will be moaning. But I shall bless Him for everything, with all my will, united to His. I shall say in union with Mary, "Fiat! Magnificat!" in the midst of the tempest, and thus I shall always have a heavenly peace in the depths of my soul.[5]

Doing God's will in daily life will sometimes hurt, but it will always bring us peace. The little way reminds me, in a frustrating moment with a family member, or as I face a battle within myself, that I *can* choose the ideal over my own base desires. I can choose holiness rather than sin. I can remain calm in the face of erroneous and even unjust behavior. I can accept the challenge of the present moment and never lose sight of the end goal: becoming a saint with the help of God's grace. My will is different than his, and I can chose to lay mine down, accept myself, my family, and my situation and know God is in control so I don't have to be.

He does a much better job running the world than I ever could, anyway.

Closing Prayer

Lord, give me the grace to surrender my desire to control people and situations, and instead to trust you. Allow me to accept your will instead of refusing it or forcing my own. Deliver me from fear about the future, and deliver me from discouragement in myself, life, and other people. Help me to know I'm not an unlovable mess but your child, gifted with both strengths and weaknesses. I trust that your grace, Lord, and not my own efforts will transform my greatest sins and my personal weaknesses. Relieve me from my anxiety about how I live my vocation, and release me from the pain of my past. I know you have not abandoned me to figure out my life on my own, but you are with me every day, intimately involved and sustaining me. Give me patience with those I love, and give me patience with myself most of all. Help me to gently apply myself to the tasks before me with great confidence in your ability to make all things well. Amen.

Discussion Questions

1. Are there any coping mechanisms described in this chapter with which you can identify? If so, which ones, and how did you develop them? How do these mechanisms affect the way you relate to your family?
2. What are a few of your strengths that help you in your marital and parenting vocations? How do your weaknesses affect your vocations? Is it difficult for you to identify your strengths and weaknesses? Why?

3. What is one aspect of dealing with your spouse and/or children that you find particularly challenging? Why?
4. Is there an area in your life that would benefit from outside help, from a spiritual director or a counselor? What is it?
5. What is one challenging surprise you've faced in parenting for which you never could have prepared?

Confession 2

I DON'T ALWAYS TAKE CARE OF MYSELF AS I SHOULD

For most of my life I have struggled to find God, to know God, to love God. . . . Now I wonder whether I have sufficiently realized that during all this time God has been trying to find me, to know me, and to love me. The question is not "How am I to find God?" but "How am I to let myself be found by him?" The question is not "How am I to know God?" but "How am I to let myself be known by God?" And, finally, the question is not "How am I to love God?" but "How am I to let myself be loved by God?" God is looking into the distance for me, trying to find me, and longing to bring me home.
—Henri Nouwen, *The Return of the Prodigal Son*

As a child, I remember my mother wore the same pair of black slip-on shoes for fourteen years. She had a beautiful home, a stable income, and disposable cash, but she wore shoes that were falling apart and had holes in them. She made the excuse she was raising kids, that she was saving money, that she didn't have the time to shop. But the real reason she never bought a new pair of shoes?

She didn't think she was worth it.

She believed Satan's lie that she was nothing, and for years she walked around with shoes split at the seams. She espoused a distorted notion of Christian "sacrifice," because she couldn't recognize her inestimable value as God's child.

My mother was a good, conscientious parent who made all four of her kids feel very special. Once, when I was sixteen, I came home crying because I felt ugly and unwanted, and she listened as I sobbed out my high school hurts. Then she dried my tears, gave me a pep talk, and shoved me out the door so I wouldn't be late for a school commitment. That night, when I returned home I found a brand new dress with matching shoes lying on my bed. Next to the gift was a note she'd written: "You're the most beautiful girl in the world." I wore that dress to school the very next day.

On top of the tremendous ability she had as a parent, my mother excels in her role as grandmother. She was there when, or soon after, all six of my children were born. When I went into labor with my second child, she bought a one-way ticket to visit us. Meaghan was born an hour before she landed, and I called her as she debarked the plane to let her know Meaghan had arrived. When she heard our new baby was a girl and we had named her after my own sister (a Dominican sister whose birth name was also Meaghan), my mom was so excited, she threw her hands up in the air and yelled, "It's a girl!" To this day, she *swears* the entire plane clapped and cheered at her announcement. We always tell our Meaghan on the day she was born, a plane brimming with people waiting on the New Orleans tarmac, the entire Murphy and Duggan clans, and her dad and me cheered for her arrival.

Each time I had a baby, my mom came to the house and stayed with us until I was back on my feet. She cooked, laundered, cleaned, and grocery shopped, as I was too hormonal and overwhelmed to do it myself. She changed dirty diapers and bought all the grandbabies an excessive amount of new clothes and toys. Since we lived far away from my parents, she begged me to send pictures of the kids all the time, because she insisted she see them every day. Every time I called to tell her one of them hit a developmental milestone, such as sleeping through the night or cutting a first tooth, she celebrated with us.

When my husband and I were first married and really poor, she would send things we needed for the kids or would randomly pay one of our bills, because she knew what it was like to live on a tight budget with many small mouths to feed. A few years ago, we relocated across the country and moved in with my mom and dad for eight months while we waited on housing. On the day we finished packing our truck to settle into our new place, she sat on the front porch and cried, mourning that we would no longer be living with her.

Her attentiveness and devotion to her family has always been a great example to me, and I credit my mother with teaching me how to be a good parent myself. She reveled in her role as a mother and continues to do so with much love and joy, even though her children are all grown and gone from her home. However, because she was so deeply wounded as a child, she wasn't able to care for herself as she deserved, especially when she was raising her own kids. She struggled with the same things I did as a new wife and mother— good eating, regular exercise, and healthy sleep habits. She didn't indulge in new clothes or anything else for herself. She kept her focus on providing for her children and saw her own needs as superfluous.

Kids follow the example set by their parents, no matter what we tell them with our words, and I carried that same struggle to take care of myself into my own marriage and parenting. Even though my mom told me every day that I was good and beautiful and kind, she didn't believe *she* was those things. There was an existential message floating in the atmosphere of our home: "I'm not good enough." My mother never said or did anything to make me feel I wasn't worthy of love, yet I still adopted that idea. As a result, I brought poor self-worth into my own marriage, and I sought to overcome it with hard work, effort, and perfection, just like my mom did.

One night, John and I pored through a box of family photos. He pulled out one of me, one month postpartum with our first child, Patrick, and exhausted. The photo captured me in front of an undecorated Christmas tree, holding newly purchased ornaments from the dollar store. I remembered the day the photo was taken: I had dragged our infant and John all over, shopping for decorations because I was hell-bent on having a magazine Christmas even on our meager income.

As if my crazy efforts to spread some holiday cheer weren't enough, I was also hell-bent on breastfeeding Patrick, which meant I pumped breast milk every two hours to stimulate production in between nursing sessions. I worked around the clock to feed Patrick, and it wasn't working. When I went for a checkup, I had lost so much weight my nurse suggested I seek testing for thyroid issues and maybe even cancer.

"I'm worried about you," she said. "It's not normal to lose weight like this after a baby. You look really tired. Are you taking care of yourself? Are you eating?"

I ignored her concern.

I wasn't taking care of myself properly. All my efforts were poured into my new home, husband, and family. I put the most basic self-care (bathing, good meals, physical exercise, sleep) on the back burner. After Patrick was born, I should have been home with my feet up; instead I was acting like a Christmas-crazed Martha Stewart. It was a lot of unnecessary pressure to put on myself, especially as a first time mom.

Years later, when I looked at the young woman in the photo, my heartstrings pulled tight. I had a deep need to do and be all things and to get everything right. I maintained such high standards for the care of my children and the management of my household. These were good things, yet the self-imposed pressure made me a wreck the first few years of our marriage. I had three babies in three years—a gift, no doubt, but I had no clue how to take care of them *and* meet my own personal needs.

Before I had children, I worked too hard and too much, I ate poorly, I went through spurts of over-the-top periods of exercise then lapsed to doing nothing, I drank too much caffeine, and I didn't rest enough. Self-care wasn't a priority before I had kids, so I had no frame of reference at all for implementing it after.

St. Josemaría Escrivá wrote, "Ask yourself many times during your day: Am I doing at this moment what I ought to be doing?"[1] For me, this was a tricky question: How much time should I spend engaging, playing, and teaching my children? How much time should I spend taking care of day-to-day duties? How much time does my spouse need? How much time is appropriate to use for myself to rest and pray? What is it I really need so that I can better serve my family?

Those last two questions were the most difficult to answer.

As a devoted Catholic, I was afraid of falling into the "all about me" mentality so prevalent in our self-obsessed culture, but I distorted the concept of "deny self" into "deny my basic needs as a human being." The pervasive and constant needs of my family combined with my insane perfectionism, and together they swallowed any inclinations toward basic self-care. I allowed all of this in the name of "sacrifice" for my family.

John's ability to take care of himself wasn't much better than my own. In college, John was a Division I athlete and, at his fastest, could run a 4:29 mile. After we married, though, John quit running because he didn't know how to manage the demands of family life and cultivate a hobby he loved. He developed a laser focus on providing for our family materially, spiritually, and emotionally, yet he neglected himself. He didn't know how to balance it all; he was a strong protector and a good provider, and all his energy went into those areas rather than into discerning and planning time for himself.

The other problem John faced was that, outside of his interest in sports, he didn't have a sense of what he actually liked to do. He was the fourth of eight children, and the group mentality of his large family meant he usually engaged in the activities in which everyone participated, without much contemplation about whether he found the activity particularly rejuvenating for himself. This wasn't his family's fault; John admits his easygoing nature didn't naturally lend itself to deep, continual reflection on what he wanted most. He brought this go-with-the-flow approach to life with him into our marriage. It was not unusual for me to ask John in the early days what movie he would like to watch or where he would like to go for dinner, and for him to look at me like I had asked him if he'd like to climb Mount Everest. He would tell me he didn't know and wouldn't offer any suggestions. It was confusing and frustrating when, days later, he'd be angry at me for selecting a movie he didn't want to watch or taking us to a restaurant he didn't enjoy.

In general, John doesn't have trouble ceding his preferences to the kids or to me. He has no qualms, for instance, about giving one of our kids the last piece of pie or handing over the remote to me. As our family grew and the opportunities for sacrifice increased, he didn't know how to see his own needs as a sign of authenticity, intelligence, and self-knowledge. He was committed to being strong for his family and taking care of our needs, yet he equated his own needs with weakness. He lived in a general state of frustration because he gave to everyone and was divorced from what he personally needed to survive and thrive in his vocation.

I was the adult child of an alcoholic, chronically prone to taking care of everyone else and lacking any frame of reference for basic, normal self-care. John was the middle child in a large family with no real sense of himself, his personal needs, and his interests. The result? We had unrealistic expectations about how the other person should meet our emotional and human needs. Our family continued to grow in size, and neither of us had the skills to respond to the great demands raising children imposed *as well as* take care of ourselves and each other. We attempted to get our needs met by serving everyone else in order to be recognized and loved. We neglected ourselves and then felt angry when others didn't see how overburdened and stressed out we were.

Right around the time when some of our interpersonal marital issues were at their peak, the bead incident with Mary Bernadette spurred me to see a counselor. I realized that sacrificing everything for my children—including my very self—wasn't really working out the way I had envisioned. I was unhappy and tired. I felt stressed and inadequate. I felt guilty about everything, even things that weren't my fault. My counselor was the first person to ever tell me I didn't have to run myself ragged in order to be holy, that holiness is actually more difficult to attain if we don't have a wellspring of reserves from which to draw. Our weekly chats convinced me it was impossible to give what I didn't have.

After I flexed my self-care muscles with a trusted advisor, John also went to counseling. By then, John had recognized that his method of sacrificing everything for our family wasn't really working either. He could see the healing and freedom I experienced from therapy, and so he humbly submitted himself to talking to someone who could help him learn about himself. For many years, we worked out our issues on our own and then—in time— we went together to a counselor to work out our issues. To this day, we both see counselors and spiritual directors separately and together whenever a sticky situation arises between us or in parenting. An objective third party helps us sort out our thoughts and feelings as well as strategize our approach to the situation.

Sacrificing Our Marriage for Our Kids Is a Bad Plan

When John and I first married, we spent most of our non-working and non-sleeping hours together, uninterrupted by the outside world. We traveled to visit friends at the beach on the weekends, spent entire afternoons in bookstores, went to the movies and out to eat, met at our favorite restaurant for margaritas, and flitted our weekends away napping in the warm sun or lounging on the couch all afternoon reading books, unfettered by responsibility. Once the children came, hammering out the details about who was going to go to the grocery store became a monumental challenge. Forget about tackling the larger interpersonal issues; who had the time?

Addressing those issues was necessary, and if those conversations didn't happen, our daily interactions became fraught with tension and negativity. For instance, I picked John up from work one afternoon, just a few years after we were married. We only had one vehicle at the time and I was always happy when 5:00 p.m. rolled around and it was time to get Daddy. I loved to tell John all about the things that happened during the day, especially the funny things the kids said or did. On this particular afternoon, there was something specific I wanted to share with him, but two of the babies in the back started whining and the other one started screaming right as John got in our SUV.

I had spent all day with the kids; I knew they were fine, that they were just overtired and hungry. I continued to tell John about my day, ignoring the din in the background, but John couldn't concentrate. It upset him that the children were unhappy. This was the first time he'd seen them all day, and he wanted to give them his attention. He snapped at me to quit talking, and I snapped back. I was hurt because I felt like John didn't want to hear about my life. John, on the other hand, felt bombarded right as he got into the car when he just wanted to ease into his evening after a long day. He was only in the car for a few minutes before we had an interaction that painted a negative shade over the entire evening.

In a week, if we had ten interactions like this and there weren't a solid number of positive ones sprinkled in between, things could begin to look pretty bleak for us as a couple. It was hard to learn how to walk the tightrope of prioritizing our marriage amid the needs and demands of our children.

And the kids were demanding.

We couldn't have overlooked them, but we struggled when it came to not overlooking each other. We knew time together was important, but finding childcare for our small herd of children so we could go on a date night and finding the extra money to do anything out of the ordinary were obstacles. We tried to be creative, and we had many in-house date nights on which we put the kids to bed early, ordered takeout, and watched a movie. These evenings were fabulous, even though nothing was as rejuvenating as slipping out the back door to take a night off from dinner and bedtime routines. After a night out on the town with John, especially early in our marriage, I'd tiptoe into the bedrooms of our sleeping children and notice their chubby hands clutching their fleece blankets. In the soft light that spilled into the kids' bedrooms, I'd watch their small chests rise and fall, and I remembered all the reasons I loved them. I realized then in the stillness of the night there was no place I'd rather be than in this house with all these people.

In those early years of marriage and parenting, I naïvely thought that as our children grew older it would be easier to find the time to date John. In a way, this is partially true, because we now have in-house babysitters. Unfortunately, those in-house babysitters have lives filled with complicated schedules and educational activities. Our older kids have us running all over town, and it's quite easy to spend our days and evenings tending to their commitments while neglecting our marriage.

John and I both came to this realization in a startling way when we committed to six weeks of marriage counseling sessions one summer, in order to learn better techniques to promote intentional dialogue. A few of the same old communication issues with which we repeatedly struggle had resurfaced, and we both wanted to glean a few pointers for healthy communication.

During our first meeting, I was so angry I could barely look at John and struggled to speak civilly to him. However, as we met each week, my anger melted away. The counselor taught us the skills she promised, and we practiced them as best we could. Her techniques were valuable tools that we still use today, but the real gift of those six weeks of counseling was the simple realization that John and I needed more one-on-one time together without interruptions. Each week, we spent several hours driving to the appointment and then back again. After our session, we always stopped for dinner to debrief. By the time we came home, we'd spent almost half a day without children and the demands of life, and we felt infinitely more affection for each other. We had forgotten what it was like to spend time together; even worse, we had forgotten how much we actually like each other.

Our commitment to counseling made me realize how easy it is for John and me to sacrifice our marriage in the name of our children. We justify skipping date nights in order to save money, yet we shell out thousands of dollars so our children can be involved in extracurricular activities, activities that run us ragged and leave us spent. We hire babysitters in order to fulfill volunteer ministry obligations for our church and yet never set aside money to go out on a date, just the two of us. We indulge our children's nightly stall tactics, which include multiple trips to the restroom, requests for water, and more than a handful of books, all of which eat away at our short window of time for conversation and connection. We give everything we have to our children—physically, emotionally, and mentally—and then are befuddled when we have nothing left to give to each other.

One day, many years from now, our six kids are going to grow up and leave us. When this happens, will John and I be strangers to each other? Will we be two people who at one time liked each other but after years of work and childrearing look at each other bewildered and skeptical?

The time we were able to spend together around our counseling sessions made us realize that we mustn't allow our children's schedules and needs dictate how we relate to each other as husband and wife. God has called John and me to holiness through the vocation of marriage; it is the avenue he uses to draw out our best selves. This requires we nurture our primary call to grow closer to God and each other, in that order. Parenting is an important, demanding aspect of our vocation, but we must put our marriage first and our children second. The best thing John and I can give to God and to our kids is a good marriage.

My kids are not a sacrament, but my marriage is.

Making Time to Make Time

During a trip to the park, I noticed a book in the bag of an acquaintance. When I asked her what she was reading, another Catholic parent leaned over and proclaimed, "I wish I had time to read."

"Maybe you just don't like to read! What is it you like to do?" I asked.

She didn't answer. She'd made her point, maybe unintentionally, but she'd communicated that she, a martyr in her family's cause, had no time for self-indulgent frivolities like reading and, I assume, any other enjoyable activity. I spot these kinds of martyr moms so easily because, if I'm not careful, I'm also one of them.

I invite you to attempt an experiment. Think about what it is you like to do. What's your first reaction when asked about a hobby? Are you excited to talk about something in which you are interested or are your first thoughts negative and dismissive?

Also try another experiment: the next time you find yourself surrounded by a group of good Christian parents, ask them about their personal pursuits, about what they like to do for rejuvenation. Then take the time to listen to the various ways people respond. Notice if anyone scoffs at your question, rolls their eyes, or makes a flip statement about how they don't have the time. In my experience, the number of people who dismiss personal pursuits outweighs the number of people who can hold a conversation about the current book they are reading or what they like to grow in their gardens or how many miles they jog a week.

We live in a frantic culture with constant stimulus overload. Couple the cultural norm of frenzied living with a Christian desire to serve our families first, and in my experience, you get parents who are overwhelmed, overburdened, and burned out. You get Catholics who desire to sacrifice everything for their families, including their very selves, but who in reality have little to give.

In an effort to hypercorrect the anthem, touted by the world, that wails, "Do whatever you want and whatever feels good," we deny ourselves in unhealthy ways and overlook our natural interests because we cannot justify the perceived self-indulgence in the face of our parental responsibilities. We can even be lax about our own prayer lives, postponing what our souls need to survive. There is always work to be done or a familial need to be filled, so we often put off what we most need—whether it is human, social, emotional, or spiritual—in order to continue our vocational work. But we can't give what we don't have, so our work suffers and lags and becomes burdensome.

Many Catholic parents, I'm afraid, are out of gas.

The other thing that prevents Catholics from proper self-care is we have so much fear tied up around the way we do what we do. Are we selfish, lazy, and indulgent parents if our children watch TV while we work out or focus on a hobby? Will our children become glazed-over robots with the verbal skills of chimpanzees if they play video games? Nursing these types of concerns fosters the tendency to make the Perfect the enemy of the Good. Our fears rule and direct our behavior, and we don't do what it takes to make sure our own needs are met. The sound choice of self-care becomes "unimportant," because fear about how our children spend their time trumps staying sane.

The problem with *never* adjusting our standards is that we force ourselves to be on top of our parenting game at all times, which eventually leads to burn out.

We walk around grumpy, without ever bathing or taking a nap or having a nice conversation with a friend, but, yay! The television hasn't been turned on and the kids aren't playing video games! Meanwhile, we are inadvertently communicating to our children we must be slaves to our standards rather than adjusting them during certain seasons or times of stress.

In Matthew's gospel, Jesus is asked the question, "Teacher, which commandment in the law is the greatest?"

Jesus replies in the following way: "You shall love the Lord, your God, with all your heart, with all your soul, and with all your mind. This is the greatest and the first commandment. The second is like it: You shall love your neighbor as yourself. The whole law and the prophets depend on these two commandments" (Mt 22:36–40).

Love God first, with everything you have, Jesus tells us. Most Catholic parents don't have trouble with this first command; we desire to love God with our whole heart and soul. The second commandment—love your neighbor *as yourself*—is more complicated, because we are aware of our selfish tendencies. We are driven by our own egos, by our own desires for comfort and power. Good-hearted Christians swim in murky water all the time; we know how easy it is to jump into a project with the intention of self-gift and quickly swim downstream in a flood of selfishness.

In order to combat our selfishness, we overcompensate. We ignore our own personal needs, and we serve others until we are at our breaking points. Jesus is clear. He doesn't say love your neighbor as the frazzled, worn down, burnt out nub of a person you've become. He says love your neighbor as yourself, as a child of God, worthy of love, quiet time, and prayer. It is only when we are kind to ourselves and when we encounter the peace of Christ that we can actually love another anyway. To offer another true compassion, we have to be compassionate with ourselves, which requires that we cultivate interior calm.[2]

One of the ways I combat my tendency to neglect myself is to make time every day to do something I enjoy. My daily life mortifies me in a million small ways, and what a pleasure it is to finally be able to open the pages of a crisp new book or sit for a moment and bang out a few thoughts on my laptop. It's renewing and fortifying to me. Unless I want to teach my children they must constantly work, I had better demonstrate what a healthy adult looks like when engaged in renewing activities.

What is it you *like* to do? Read? Write? Paint? Dance? Exercise? Take photographs? What? What is it that *interests* you? Pick something and cultivate that, every day and in some small way. Developing our own personal interests is *not* selfish; it's actually good for us! It's right living, makes us better people, and fulfills God's intention for our lives. And cultivating our own hobbies reduces the likelihood we will resent another person who takes care of himself or herself in a healthy manner. We won't find ourselves making off-handed remarks such as "Must be nice" or "Wish I had the time" to those engaged in their own personal pursuits. Instead, we can share our own personal experiences of our hobbies and can support and encourage other parents in the trenches, parents who, just like us, are trying to do the best they can.

Lessons from St. Ignatius

I became interested in St. Ignatius of Loyola a few summers ago when I picked up his autobiography and discovered he was like me, someone who had to learn the importance of taking care of himself in order to do God's will more fully. Ignatius was not a naturally balanced person but one who struggled with extremes. The first line of his autobiography illustrates Ignatius's intensity: "Until the age of twenty-six he was a man given up to the vanities of the world, and his chief delight used to be in the exercise of arms, with a great and vain desire to gain honor."[3]

Ignatius was a worldly man who longed to be a famous soldier. He was also predisposed to aggressive behavior. One author notes that Ignatius is probably the only saint to have a police record for a "serious desire to inflict harm on his enemies" during a nighttime brawl.[4]

After his conversion, Ignatius struggled with an immoderate approach to spiritual practices. For instance, Ignatius spent some alone time in a cave outside of his home town, where he implemented a series of severe penances including "fasting, praying for hours on end, and allowing his hair and fingernails to grow, as a way of surrendering his previous desire for a pleasing appearance."[5] His physical depravation was so radical, he felt depressed, weak, and even suicidal. He finally realized his extreme austerity prevented him from serving others in the way God desired, and he adjusted his practices accordingly.

Ignatius of Loyola's path to sainthood was peppered with evaluation and reevaluation of practices he thought were good. At one point in his priestly life, he temporarily suspended saying daily Mass because he experienced the "gift of tears," a tendency to weep during profound religious experiences. The gift of tears exhausted him and impaired his vision during the Consecration, so for a brief time he gave up saying Mass. He didn't plow through his responsibilities despite his condition (like I might have done). He didn't force a solution or walk around irritated and yelling at people because he was so emotionally drained from Mass. He simply took a step back, without any guilt and without any explanation to bystanders. He didn't suspend his eucharistic responsibilities forever, just for enough time to renew his body, mind, and soul so that he could continue his important work.[6]

Ignatius implemented a general ruling principle that encouraged good habits of food, rest, and exercise so he and the rest of his Jesuit priests could work effectively. He rejected the popular and often extreme religious penances of his time, such as the wearing of hair shirts and extreme fasting, and he encouraged the Jesuits to be of sound body and mind.[7] If the founder of a religious order who sent priests to evangelize every corner of the world saw fit to encourage good sleep, eating, exercise, prayer, and personal habits, why should we feel it is acceptable to ignore our own basic human needs? There are seasons in life (think, three children under the age of three) when extra self-care is going to be more difficult, but it is not unreasonable for a sleep-deprived mom to go take a nap even though there is laundry piled high or dinner isn't planned (you'll figure it out, I promise). It is not unreasonable for an overwhelmed dad to take a siesta on Saturday afternoon even though the lawn isn't mowed or his daughter needs help with a science project. It is not unreasonable for married parents to leave children with a babysitter so they can sneak out for a date night or meet friends for a beer or cup of coffee. Our children will not forget us, nor will some deep parental bond be broken, if we prioritize marriage and go out for a few hours. Choosing a refreshing outlet enables us to accept and delight in the reality of being human. We are not just cogs in a spinning, meaningless wheel. We are beings endowed with humanity, we are part of creation, and it is good to reflect and acknowledge our part in the grand scheme of that beautiful existence. If we are always on the go and burned out with our work, we have no energy to revel in the reality of who and what we are. Self-care allows us to appreciate what it means—even if we sometimes feel burdened by it—to be a human.

Closing Prayer

Lord, you've given me an important job in this world as a parent to my children, and I take this job seriously, sometimes to the detriment of my marriage and my own spiritual, human, and emotional needs. Forgive me for the times I've put my children ahead of my spouse, and forgive me for my own self-neglect. Give me the grace to place the Sacrament of Marriage in its proper order, and help me to tend to my human needs for prayer, food, sleep, and self-care. Amen.

Discussion Questions

1. Do you have a tendency to be moderate or immoderate in self-care? Why? Were your own parents good examples of this? What did they do well, and what needed improvement?
2. What are some hobbies you enjoy? Do you still engage in those hobbies? Why or why not?

3. When are you most tempted to neglect yourself? Why? What are some safeguards you can implement to prevent gross self-negligence?

4. Do you prioritize your faith, or do you let yourself get caught in the rhythms of daily life without taking time to grow in your faith? What is one way you can be more intentional about your faith this week?

5. How do you communicate with your spouse? Does that need to change? How do you maintain your marriage as a priority amid the demands of life?

Confession 3

I DON'T KNOW HOW TO KEEP MY KIDS CATHOLIC

Humbly let go. Let go of trying to do, let go of trying to control, let go of my own way, let go of my own fears. Let God blow His wind, His trials, and oxygen for joy's fire. Leave the hand open and be. Be at peace. Bend the knee and be small and let God give what God chooses to give because He only gives love.

—Ann Voskamp, *One Thousand Gifts*

I'm a cradle Catholic, and, while I don't have a falling-to-the-ground conversion story like St. Paul does, my Catholic education, especially my study of theology at Saint Mary's College, cemented my faith. A deep reading of the Church's teachings through the various writings of the saints and the papal encyclicals convinced me that the Catholic Church contained truth. There was no question when John and I married and started a family about whether we would practice Catholicism. We both agreed to teach the faith to our children as well as create a vibrant Catholic culture within our home.

Reading Jesus' invitation in Luke 18 to leave all and follow him motivated me to reject the culture's lie that true happiness comes in service of the self, and I wanted to teach my children to do the same. I desired to emulate Mother Mary in the way she formed Jesus in her own domestic church and to follow what the *Catechism* says about our grave and primary moral duty to instruct our children: "Parents should initiate their children at an early age into the mysteries of the faith of which they are the 'first heralds' for their children. They should associate them from their tenderest years with the life of the Church" (CCC, 2225).

My children's moral education and spiritual formation was of primary importance, and I felt armed and ready for the task. They would know and receive instruction on the precepts and moral teachings of the Church; I would teach them how to pray; they would benefit from faithful, regular exposure to the sacraments; and we would offer help as they discerned their proper vocation as children of God (see CCC, 2221, 2226).

As a teacher myself, I longed for a holistic elementary and secondary education that would form my children's wills and consciences and aid them in deeper understanding of God, themselves, and how to use their innate gifts to serve the world. I imagined immersing them in the sacred beauty of our faith—teaching them about liturgical feast days, the rote prayers of the Church, and how to worship at Mass. I had visions of coordinated feast day meals to honor our obscure saints. I imagined my small brood of children, dressed in matching pajamas and holding lighted candles and their First Holy Communion rosaries—the ones blessed by St. John Paul II and stored after each use—while they sat on comfortable, coordinated throw pillows reciting the Mysteries of the Rosary. The mere thought of my children's soft, sweet voices as they repeated the memorized prayers of Our Lady caused me to tear up.

Except when it came time for any kind of actual faith formation, the scene I longed for wasn't what I imagined—not even a little. The reality looked much, much different. We dutifully brought our children to church, for instance, and there they behaved as children do—like crazy people. John and I have a few favorite stories we pull out of our parenting arsenal when we're looking to entertain friends with an *I can't believe my kid did this to me* kind of story. Like the time our toddler shut off all the lights in the church in the middle of Pentecost Mass, and the bishop joked it was because of the Holy Spirit and not the handsy two-year-old who'd played with the light switch. Or the time a random stranger grabbed our baby so I could collect the toddler who was crawling up the aisle on all fours, tongue out, panting like a dog, while the other three school-aged children stood and walked fully erect across the pews, tossing hymnals as they went. Or the time our five-year-old tripped on the pew, gashing the corner of his eye so deeply he required stitches, all the while issuing an ear-piercing death cry. Or (and this is John's personal favorite) the time our eight-year-old daughter slapped her younger sister across the face in the middle of Easter Sunday Mass, just because. Or (my favorite) the time the two preschool-aged children escaped from me while I had my eyes closed in prayer, and a male parishioner had to help me collect them from the men's room, where one of them was army-crawling back and forth underneath the stalls.

All the time I spent in quiet prayer, Bible studies, yearly retreats, and weekly visits to the Adoration chapel before marriage morphed into minute-by-minute survival to keep the toddler alive and off the altar. Where I once sat alone and unhindered in prayer before

marriage, my vocation after demanded jostling a thir-
ty-pound child while wearing ill-fitting heels and sweat-
ing because I had just coaxed the twenty-three month
old from under the kneeler. To further my disillusion-
ment, the moments of quiet, pious instruction I intended
never happened. John and I felt as if we were trying to
teach the faith to velociraptors rather than preschoolers.

As the children grew older, things got even more
complicated. We were confounded by their evolving
anti-church attitudes. Almost every time we made them
put on a suit or a dress, drove them across town, and
situated them in a pew for sixty minutes, they were dis-
gruntled and disinterested, despite a donut bribe for
good behavior.

*Shouldn't this whole Mass thing be easier for everyone
involved?* we wondered.

As if the struggle to get our children to Mass wasn't
enough, once we were there, we then spent sixty minutes in tremendous anxiety over their behavior. We worried about what other people would think. We worried
we were distracting other parishioners and that other
people would question our discipline tactics if one of
the kids decided to throw an epic temper tantrum in
the middle of the Consecration. (It didn't help when
one weekend John and I actually heard a husband
mutter to his wife he believed our oldest son needed a
"whooping.")

Beyond my concern about whether it was normal
for the preschooler to request to use the restroom in the
middle of the Prayers of the Faithful every week, our
deepest worry revolved around whether they were ever
going to understand the importance of Sunday Mass
and the richness of the Catholic Church. We fretted they
would not know the real reason we brought them to

church, they would reject the Church's teachings, and they would come to believe the whole Sunday Mass thing was a pointless waste of time. What if our kids never embraced the faith as their own; what if they left the Church for good as soon as they had the opportunity to do so?

This compulsive worry caused my husband and me to do adopt some unreasonable parenting practices. Instead of simply redirecting crazy kid behavior at Mass, we decided to eradicate their silliness. We became Mass Nazis, removing rewards and toys and any other privileges we could think of whenever our children's behavior was too much. We threatened and cajoled and bribed and left Mass each week exhausted and in great need of family naps. No wonder all my kids hated church! It was a sixty-minute power struggle in which we were determined to hammer a love for the Church into our children's hearts.

We didn't have a good understanding of what was realistic for our children's religious instruction given their developmental stages. John and I naïvely believed the six- and seven-year-old would sit in rapt attention as we instructed them on the mechanics of the Rosary or as we explained the theological concept of transubstantiation. During the course of our lectures, we were befuddled and frustrated when fights broke out among the siblings and the toddler peed on the sofa. We knew we wanted to convey the faith, but it was unrealistic to think our toddler would be able to comprehend transubstantiation at Sunday Mass. Sure, I could point to Jesus on the Cross and talk to him about Love Incarnate, but sitting quietly in the pew for sixty minutes because Jesus becomes our food was an impossible task for him.

It was also impractical for us to expect we would be able to sit in monastic-like prayer during Sunday Mass when we had small children by our sides. The likelihood we would have to deal with an explosive diaper bomb from not one but two different kids far outweighed the likelihood of a personal mountaintop experience. We didn't know yet that God was using these moments of self-sacrifice during Mass to form *us* in our vocations. We suspected our children misbehaved on purpose, just to make us miserable, when they were simply acting their age. We expected them to sit in the pew and be quiet and still, though, as I realized much later, most children can't acquire this skill until they have reached the age of reason. It doesn't mean we give up teaching them what's happening on the altar or redirecting misbehavior when they're young, but I had to learn to accept "good enough" Mass behavior rather than "perfect."

Our impossibly high expectations meant John and I felt mostly defeated and discouraged when we attempted Mass, nightly family prayer, reading a small story from *The Lives of the Saints*, or a liturgical celebration with our kids because we were almost always met with insurmountable problems (also known as normal kid quandaries). Our attempts at family bonding were met with shouts of "She hit me!" "You're squishing me!" or "Patrick called me ugly!" instead of cries of "I love being Catholic!" "Thank you for loving us, Mom and Dad!" or "Talk about the best parents ever!" for which we hoped. What we intended to be a formative, bonding activity for the family—like praying the Rosary before a fire in the middle of Advent—often ended in someone being sent to their room or an adult losing patience. (And honestly, once a parent starts yelling in the middle of the Rosary, the point has been lost.) We romanticized how we'd like things to be, but we were stuck in the reality of chronic imperfection—our own and our kids'. All the drama caused us to want to give up because even small things like grace before meals seemed too hard.

Whitewashed Tombs or Free to Choose?

One of the greatest things lacking in our presentation of the Catholic faith to our children was a respect for our children's freedom, especially the freedom for them to behave in age-appropriate ways. John and I had to learn the importance of accepting the limits of our children's behavior, given their ages, in order to make Mass and family prayer time a better experience. Accepting the kids' developmental capabilities lessened our irritation with them and removed the desire to implement over-the-top disciplinary efforts. The fact is—even if we couldn't always appreciate it—it *was* age appropriate for our toddler to throw his sippy cup across the pew or for the four-year-old to try to bathe in the holy water. Allowing normal, kidlike behavior didn't mean we abdicated our responsibility to teach them how to behave at Church or in the middle of a family Rosary, but it did mean we needed to learn not to be so angry and surprised by their antics. Instead of continuing our earlier approach of hammering developmental tendencies out of our kids, we redirected the behavior as best we could and worked with the kids according to their ability and temperaments.

We didn't land on this approach overnight, of course. We learned the importance of working with and not against our children's aptitudes over time and in a roundabout way. Through counseling, John and I discovered we sometimes have a tendency to perform in a way others expect, even if internally we don't want to or we feel resentful. When presented with another's request, we don't always feel free to give a real yes or a real no; we feel like we need to do what other people want to keep the peace or make someone else happy, even if it means sacrificing our own peace and happiness. We are sometimes like the scribes and the Pharisees Jesus critiqued when he said in Matthew 23:27, "Woe to you, scribes and Pharisees, you hypocrites. You are like whitewashed tombs, which appear beautiful on the outside, but inside are full of dead men's bones and every kind of filth." We looked good externally because we did what others wanted, though internally we were full of resentment and bitterness.

Becoming aware of this relational tendency made us reflect on how we wanted to raise our own children, especially as it applied to Catholicism. Did we want our kids to be whitewashed tombs who cooperated with our requests to be good little Catholics but felt coerced? Did we just want them to do what we said because we said it, or did we want to engage them in discussions about the faith so that they could claim it as their own? Did we want our kids to sit in the pew each Sunday, well behaved and good-looking—but inside to be filled with disinterest, anger, and resentment?

The *Catechism of the Catholic Church* states, "Freedom is exercised in relationships between human beings. Every human person, created in the image of God, has the natural right to be recognized as a free and responsible being. All owe to each other this duty of respect. The right to the exercise of freedom, especially in moral and religious matters, is an inalienable requirement of the dignity of the human person" (*CCC*, 1738). As our children grew, we decided that we needed to follow this teaching and that we would rather allow our children the freedom to act their age than expect them to put their developmental tendencies on hold for sixty minutes each week. We wanted to allow our kids the freedom to tell us if they hated going to Church so we could actually engage them in conversation rather than have them sit docile and obedient in our pew for eighteen years and then discard their faith in college. We decided to take a leap of faith by respecting their developmentally appropriate behavior and hoped that our respect for their freedom would motivate them to choose the faith for themselves one day.

This is definitely a messier way of parenting. It means we spend a lot of time acknowledging the emotions and challenges they experience. It means we affirm our kids in the difficulties they face, and when appropriate, we share our own faith struggles with them. While we will always require them to attend Sunday Mass and fulfill religious obligations while they live under our roof, we try not to focus too much on the externals while we're there; instead we delve into the unseen parts of each child's faith journey. We didn't lower our standards for our children's faith formation. Rather, we are more realistic about what their faith formation looks like.

To be clear, our children's faith formation isn't always pretty, convenient, or peaceful.

Is there anything in Catholic family life that is?

Surrendering My Fear and Focusing on Fidelity

When I first became a mom, I didn't realize I had so much fear tied up in how I presented the faith to our children. I worried I was not catechizing them well enough, and I worried about the chaotic nature of our family prayer time (if we could even figure out how to organize family prayer at all). I worried we weren't teaching our children enough about their faith, that we weren't reading to them enough from the books of the saints or the Bible. I worried they didn't understand the sacraments in a deep, personal way. I worried our children wouldn't know that Jesus Christ becomes our food for us to eat in the Eucharist, and I worried they wouldn't have the rote prayers of the Catholic Church memorized when they needed them most.

I still worry about all these things sometimes, because I long for my children to know God like I do, to recognize that the only perfect happiness they will ever find is with him. A few years ago, however, I had a spiritual revelation, which significantly lessoned my anxiety about reaching the end goal of adult children who practice Catholicism. At the time, I was worried I was failing in my duties as a Catholic parent, and I needed some clarification from my spiritual director on whether I had taken a very wrong turn. I also had recently spent several days reading and praying over Mark 8:1–9, and I felt frustrated by the turn of events in the gospel story. Mark writes:

> In those days when there again was a great crowd without anything to eat, he summoned the disciples and said, "My heart is moved with pity for the crowd, because they have been with me now for three days and have nothing to eat. If I send them away hungry to their homes, they will collapse on the way, and some of them have come a great distance." His disciples answered him, "Where can anyone get enough bread to satisfy them here in this deserted place?" Still he asked them, "How many loaves do you have?" "Seven," they replied. He ordered the crowd to sit down on the ground. Then, taking the seven loaves he gave thanks, broke

them, and gave them to his disciples to distribute, and they distributed them to the crowd. They also had a few fish. He said the blessing over them and ordered them distributed also. They ate and were satisfied. They picked up the fragments left over— seven baskets. There were about four thousand people.

Let me emphasize for a moment how incredible it was to me the people had been with Jesus for three days and they didn't have anything to eat. I have six children and spend a significant part of my days, weeks, and months securing food and feeding it to the masses. It is a fundamental part of my job, the nourishment of the serial eaters with whom I live, so the fact that Jesus was on a mountaintop with about four thousand people and there was no food for three days boggled my mind. I can't go thirty minutes before someone shouts, "Moooooom, I'm hungry!" How did Jesus and the people last three days?

It also annoyed me that Jesus knew the people were way past hunger; we know they were in great need of food because he tells his disciples, "Look, we have to feed these people or they will collapse on the way home." I was a little outraged over this situation, so I dragged myself to Father's office and once we were face to face, I expressed my concerns to him: "How could Jesus get away with that? Didn't he see the people were in physical need? OK, so he was feeding them spiritually, but we are humans first! How could he ignore their need for food? Weren't they driving him crazy with complaints? Trust me, I know what it's like to be around hangry people. It's stressful and miserable! Why did he make them wait—three whole days—before he performed a miracle? It makes no sense."

Father listened without judgment and then asked me, "Do you feel like the hungry people in the parable? Is Jesus asking you to wait for a miracle?"

His question caught me off guard. I stared up at the ceiling, arms crossed over my chest, still annoyed by the entire no food on the mountain for three days scenario.

"Yes!" I said finally. "I feel like Jesus has dragged me up on a mountaintop just to make me wait for . . . what? Even though I have John, I feel alone raising these kids and guiding their faith lives to the best of my ability. I worry I'm failing them. I'm stepping out of my boat, just like Peter did when Jesus called him to walk on water, and I'm drowning. And then Jesus decides to make me wait three days before he feeds me!"

Father and I talked for an hour about the scripture passage and about how I felt so unsure in my efforts to raise Catholic children. I told him I felt abandoned by God in shepherding these kids. I cried the entire time, and before I left Father said, "You haven't prayed over the feeding of the four thousand people enough. You need to revisit that scripture passage this upcoming month. You need to pray for more insight," he suggested. "I don't think you've got it all yet."

A few days after I met with Father, a close friend of mine slipped me a book. After she had read it herself, my friend knew I would like the book's message, so she ordered me a copy. Imagine my surprise then, when on a Saturday morning, nestled in my quiet bedroom, sipping a steaming cup of coffee, I read the following:

> Just like the disciples I see this huge throng of people to feed—this seeming impossibility. The shaping of souls and raising of children, the mopping of floors, washing of dishes, bandaging of scraped knees and hearts and worries, the teaching and admonishing

and loving and doling out of myself. It's all too
much. There are six children in this home; there is
one of me. I fall to my knees and I cry out to God.
We're a throng of hungry people in the desert, and
I'm supposed to feed them. On an ordinary Monday,
I am in need of a miracle of biblical proportions.[1]

I took pause. This author just described my situation, she just described *me*. I had used these exact words only a few days before to explain to Father how overwhelmed I felt! Six hungry kids? Check. A houseful of responsibility? Check. The emotional reactions of various human beings (including me) that could easily measure a 9.7 on the Richter scale? Check. A bumbling parent desperately in need of a miracle? Check.

It isn't that I have nothing, exactly. I have my little
basket. I can read aloud pretty well. I'm good at
organizing things on paper. I can make a decent pot
of chili and I know how to push a vacuum. I love
my children with all of my being and I have a real
desire to watch them grow to love and serve Him.
I don't really have any idea how I'm supposed to
tackle everything ahead of me in this day, this year,
this decade when that's all I've got. It's just a couple
loaves of bread and a few fish.
        Apparently, that's all he needs.[2]

I had been looking at this difficult situation in the wrong light. I felt so overwhelmed and frustrated with parenting because I mistakenly thought *I* was responsible for the miracle, I thought my efforts alone would ensure the raising of good, Catholic children. I thought it was my job to produce educated citizens capable of serving their neighbor.

But it's not my job to do those things; it's Jesus' job. My job is to show up with my loaves and fishes, to come prepared and do my best and let Jesus take care of the rest. All the self-induced stress I had placed on myself to present the Catholic faith to my children perfectly was wasted emotional energy. My imperfect efforts to form my family were good enough. I could take my worry about producing Catholic children and lay it at the foot of the Cross. Jesus calls me to show up with my loaves and fishes, to be prepared and ready to work. I want to do what he asks, but I am not expected to produce a miracle. I don't have that kind of power! I'm called to give my all, be faithful, and educate my children to the best of my ability, but it's not in my wheelhouse to produce children who love and are faithful to the Church.

Jesus faced a very imperfect scenario on the mountaintop. He went up there and had no way to physically feed the people; this wasn't an ideal situation. In a perfect world, maybe Jesus would have brought a caterer with him so the people could go through the buffet line whenever they got hungry, but that's not what happened. In real life the hungry crowd followed Jesus because they wanted to be near him. No one planned, no one thought ahead about what they would need, and no one brought extra food. That day on the mountain, though, there was a young boy who had a few supplies. He offered what he carried to the group and Jesus produced a miracle: he fed four thousand starving people on a few loaves and fishes. The scenario wasn't perfect, but the miracle was.

How often is family life like this? How often are we faced with moody children or a difficult spouse when we want to pray together as a family? How often are our attempts to do something formative met with complaints or criticism or even backlash? The truth is, forming Catholic kids is not going to be easy. It's going to take hard work and prayer and trust in God. It's going to take humility. It's going to require that we surrender those idealistic visions of Catholic family life we may have and accept the real family we have sitting right in front of us. God does not owe us perfectly behaved children during Sunday Mass and moments of prayerful ecstasy just because we decide to raise a Catholic family. We are not entitled to a life of ease just because we have committed to raising Catholic kids. On the contrary, we've picked a narrow road in a world that will criticize us, questions us, and suggest a different route. Our best bet is to roll up our sleeves, get to work, and trust Jesus to fill in the gaps of even the most difficult of situations so long as we offer our simple loaves and fishes, an offering that is not perfect but that is good enough. The truth is, we aren't responsible for whether our children become Catholics.

Success isn't the goal.

Miracle making isn't the goal.

Our goal is to discern the path God is calling us to and then to do all we can to stay on the path and teach our children to do the same. It isn't our job to make our kids stay Catholic. It is our job is to show up with the necessary supplies and to be faithful. If we want to really win at Catholic parenting, we need to go to the mountaintop with our loaves and fishes, sit at the feet of Jesus, and patiently wait for the miracle.

I'll meet you there.

We Must Never Neglect Our Own Faith Life

Of course, trusting God with the end result doesn't mean we take a vacation from hard work. Entrusting the end result to God requires we redouble our own efforts to become saints ourselves. St. Charles Borromeo once said, "Be sure that you first preach by the way you live. If you do not, people will notice that you say one thing, but live otherwise, and your words will bring only cynical laughter and a derisive shake of the head."[3] Borromeo's words encourage us to practice what we preach, which is especially important when instructing children in the Catholic faith. My kids are expert hypocrite detectors, and if I ever adopt a "Do as I say, not as I do" attitude, they are quick to point out my double standard. Then they ignore me.

It's a grave temptation for Catholic parents to become so focused on forming our families in the faith we neglect our own faith. If we aren't careful, our families become the little pet projects we throw ourselves into "improving" and "guiding." Perhaps we've sat through entire lectures or homilies on prayer and our only takeaway is a renewed effort to get our kids or our spouse to pray more. Perhaps we've shoved books on the spiritual life into the hands of our family members, books we've never bothered to read ourselves. Perhaps we've commented on our spouse's "lack" of Catholic identity and the failures we notice in his or her spiritual life. Perhaps we've complained about our second grader's refusal to memorize his Act of Contrition, the disinterest our child in middle school exhibits regarding her upcoming Confirmation, and the general lack of reference and piety in prayer we see in our kids. What's missing in our critique of our family member's spiritual performance is an honesty about the struggles *we* face in committing ourselves to daily prayer! If we truly want our families to care for their own souls, we must ensure we are dedicated to the same. We must make daily prayer and frequent reception of the sacraments a priority. We must cultivate spiritual friendships, read books on the spiritual life, go on retreat, write in our journal, and communicate to our families in a million other ways other than our words that our relationship with God is the most important thing in the world to us. And we must be very careful about critiquing our family member's faith life, especially if our own is not in order.

Fr. Jaques Philippe addresses this very thing when he writes,

> At times of struggle we need also to recall the conversion we should be concerned about is not our neighbor's but our own. Only if we take our own conversion seriously do we stand any chance of seeing our neighbor converted too. This point of view is realistic and encouraging. We have little real influence on other people, and our attempts to change them have only a very slight chance of success, since most of the time we want them to change in line with our criteria and aims more than God's. If we are concerned first with our own conversion, however, we have more hope of making a difference. It does more good to seek to reform our hearts than to reform the world or the Church. Everyone will benefit. . . .
>
> We shouldn't become indifferent. Just the opposite. The holier we are, the more we will suffer due to the evil and sin and in the world. But external evil only harms us to the degree we react badly to it, by fear, worry, discouragement, sadness, giving up, rushing to apply hasty solutions that don't solve anything, judging.[3]

So we can quit worrying and wringing our hands about the spiritual poverty of our family members, especially when our own souls are so impoverished. Instead, we can encourage those around us when we see them doing good; and, when worry seizes us, we can refocus on our own spiritual efforts.[4]

And what does a commitment to daily prayer look like? Jesus gives a perfect example throughout his entire public ministry. In Mark 1:35 we read about him rising before dawn to spend time with God the Father. He held vigil all night on the eve before he named his twelve Apostles (see Luke 6:12). And littered throughout the scriptures, we see his dedication to recollected silence (see Mark 6:46 and Luke 5:16; 9:18, 28; and 21:37).

As Fr. Thomas Dubay points out, "If anyone on our planet were to have a reason to relegate prayer to a secondary place in his daily round of duties, one might think it to be the man who has six billion people to be concerned about."[5]

But he didn't.

If Jesus got up early to pray, to spend time with his heavenly Father, why do we think we're too busy? We can't let our spouses, our kids, and our schedules excuse us from daily prayer. Our prayer life must be non-negotiable, fundamental to our days and existence, a commitment we prioritize over everything else.

Powerful is the example of Catholic parent who regularly makes time to pray on his or her own and who participates in the sacraments. If we truly want our children to care and feed their souls, we must ensure we are dedicated to tending our own. Do you want to your kids to love and practice the Catholic faith?

Decide right now to sit at the feet of Jesus every day.

The danger of excessive nagging is that our words may begin to fall on indifferent ears. Our example, however, may lead to our true desire: Catholic kids. And if our example fails? The regular contact with God in prayer will change *us*.

It's Not about Me

A few years ago, Mary Bernadette and I were nestled in the church pew listening to instructions on how to proceed so the one hundred and fifty children present might receive their First Reconciliation in the most efficient and effective manner possible. We were there for Mary Bernadette, as she was one of the one hundred and fifty children, and as I sat watching the setting sun dance across the walls of the church, the light colored a buttery yellow I found comforting, I couldn't believe we were here, and now was her time.

After the prayers and the gospel reading, we were instructed to get in line. Someone had taped six different colored construction paper hearts around the church, each colored heart corresponding with a heart pinned to one of the six priests. Mary Bernadette and I sought out the sign with the blue heart on it and we waited while the priest spoke to each and every child in a makeshift confessional situated out in the open.

I could easily see the children sitting before the priest, a Benedictine monk in a black habit who sported a beard as white as Santa Claus's. As each child spoke his or her sins, the monk leaned in to listen and then spoke ever so softly to the child. After a few minutes, it was Mary Bernadette's turn to go. The lady directing the line signaled her, and she walked toward the priest. I watched her as she wandered away from me and left me alone in the line, her blond hair gleaming in the sunlight that poured through the windows and her soft brown boots clipping the marble floors, and thought, *It's*

*between you and God, kid. All these years, I've brought you
to him, but now it's up to you.*

In parenting, you spend so much time teaching and
preparing your children for life, for basic things such as
good hygiene and manners, and then other important
things such as receiving the sacraments. You bring them
to Mass every Sunday and teach them their prayers,
and then, all of a sudden, one day your kids are supposed to actually *do* what you've been training them
to do. They're supposed to want to receive the sacraments and practice their faith. We parents spend our
entire time teaching and talking and professing to our
children the Catholic faith, but one day those kids are
going to actually have to choose it for themselves. We
can't make them or strong-arm them or implement any
other tactical measure to get them to do the right thing.
They have to decide.

That night, as Mary Bernadette went forward to
receive her First Reconciliation, I felt consoled by this
thought. John and I can bring Mary Bernadette to Christ
through the sacraments, through family prayer, through
religious education classes, and through acting as good,
albeit imperfect, witnesses. We can work with all our
might to expose her to the Catholic faith, to teach her
the only life worth living is one in which God is our best
friend, but in the end, it's up to her.

I pray she chooses well. Honestly? I would be dev-
astated if Mary Bernadette or any one of my children
decided to leave the faith. But in the final analysis, it will
be between Mary Bernadette and God.

It was never between Mary Bernadette and me.

Closing Prayer

Lord, the job you've given me—to imbue my children with the Catholic faith—is the most important one I have as a parent. I'm sometimes overwhelmed and anxious about the nature and girth of the task, but I trust you will not leave me to accomplish the work alone. Give my spouse and me the grace to be faithful in bringing our children to you in the sacraments, no matter what kind of obstacles we face. Help us to have reasonable expectations for them as they explore and practice Catholicism, and enable us to respond appropriately to their developmental, spiritual, and emotional needs. Help me persevere in the face of challenges that arise as we bring our children to you, protect my kids from the dangers of the world, and let their minds and hearts be guided by the goodness found in your teachings.

Let me never place forming my children about my own commitment to you, and help me surrender my desire to control the faith lives of those I love. Lavish your grace upon my poor example; teach me to be a good teacher. I entrust my children into your hands and the hands of your mother, knowing that, even more than I do, you both want them to love you. Amen.

Discussion Questions

1. Are you and your spouse on the same page when it comes to raising Catholic kids? Do you work with or against your spouse? How could you support your spouse more in his or her efforts to form your children? Where should you back off?
2. Did you have preconceived notions about what it would be like to raise Catholic kids? Were your ideas accurate or not?

3. What is the biggest challenge you face as a Catholic parent?
4. Are you tempted to manage your spouse's or your children's spiritual life? Why or why not?
5. How is your prayer life? What is one Catholic practice or devotion you love? Does your family know you love it? When, where, or how do you practice that devotion in everyday life?

Confession 4

I DON'T LIKE WATCHING MY CHILDREN SUFFER

> God, grant me the serenity to accept the things I
> cannot change, the courage to change the things I
> can, and the wisdom to know the difference. Amen.
> —Serenity Prayer

About ten days after our oldest child, Patrick, was born,
I sat on our red, overstuffed couch trying to nurse him.
My mom and John were sitting across from me, and as
I stared at my beautiful newborn I confessed to the both
of them I was worried Patrick wasn't eating enough.

"He's thriving," my mom said, confused about my
concern.

"Colleen, he's fine," John insisted, chalking my
worry up to a form of newly developed maternal OCD.

"No, he's not. I think he's dehydrated. He's sleeping
too much, and he's not having enough dirty diapers. I
think I need to bring him to the lactation nurse at the
hospital so she can look at him and tell me if I'm doing
something wrong."

"If that will make you feel better, then you should
bring him, but I think he's fine," my mother said.

The next morning, I drove over to the hospital and
found the lactation specialist who had helped me after

Patrick's birth. I listed my concerns as the nurse stripped Patrick down.

"Let's have a look and see if your mama has a right to be worried," she said to Patrick when I finished speaking.

She placed my baby's naked, screaming body onto the cold metal scale and waited for the digital number face to blink. After a moment or two, the numbers on the screen confirmed my suspicion. Although he was born well over eight pounds at birth, the scale let us know Patrick's weight was down more than two pounds, significantly more than the appropriate 7 to 10 percent infants naturally shed. My nurse freaked out.

"Colleen, he's lost too much weight! He needs a bottle, right now."

The nurse grabbed my baby from the scale. "That's a good boy," she cooed as she shoved a bottled of formula into his mouth. I wanted to vomit but cried instead, thoughts racing: *How had I allowed him to lose so much weight? Why wasn't the nursing working? What was I doing wrong?*

The nurse tried to comfort me.

"Don't worry, Colleen," she said, grabbing my hand with her free one and squeezed it. "We're going to get him working again. You have to follow my feeding instructions, but Patrick is going to be OK," she said, patting my back. "We're gonna figure this out."

Patrick, nestled in the nurse's arms, sucked down that formula like it was his job. The poor darling was starving. I sat on the couch, feeling like a complete loser. I had already failed the most important job I had as a new mom: to feed my baby.

After Patrick ate, we burped, fed him, got him dressed, and then the nurse spent the next hour with me showing me how to properly breastfeed Patrick—again.

"You nurse him first, Colleen. Make sure he gets enough of that delicious milk from you and when you finish, if he's still hungry, you top him off with some of your pumped milk or some formula. It's dangerous for him to lose so much weight, Colleen. He's not getting enough food. You have to supplement him with formula until we get this nursing thing figured out."

My nurse also insisted I bring him to our pediatrician immediately for monitoring until Patrick picked up weight. I followed every single one of her suggestions. I also did whatever my doctor suggested and anyone else who had a "handy" tip or two on how to breastfeed effectively. For months, I visited with the lactation specialist as often as my budget would afford and attended La Leche League meetings. I read every book on nursing and on how to overcome feeding issues, and I implemented every suggestion just about anyone had to offer: I pumped in between feedings, I took natural supplements, I didn't use pacifiers, and I even used a supplemental feeding system. None of it worked. Patrick wasn't gaining weight, and I wasn't producing enough to keep him healthy.

I agonized about the best way to feed the baby, and, when my worry failed to produce results, I badgered John about what I should do. I woke him up in the middle of the night for moral support during late night feeding sessions. I cried from the painful infections that caused me to bleed into the breast pump. I cried when I had to give Patrick a bottle, fearful my son wouldn't be attached me to me, his primary caregiver.

It was the lactation consultant who eventually encouraged me to call it quits. I had dragged Patrick to her office one morning—again—for advice when she said it: "You know, honey, you're not a failure if you give your baby a bottle. You've tried your best to nurse him, and it's not working. I don't know what else you can do. I'm worried about you. You look too thin and very tired. I don't think you're taking care of yourself very well, and I think you need to be realistic—you've tried to nurse, and it didn't work. Formula-feeding Patrick does not make you a bad mother."

Tears rolled down my cheeks, and I nodded my acknowledgements. I sobbed the entire drive home. I wanted to nurse Patrick, and while I knew the lactation consultant was right and I wasn't a failure as a woman and a mother, I still felt like one. I believed—and still do—nursing was the best thing for a baby. I was willing to make the sacrifices to give Patrick my breast milk, but nothing I did worked. I was confused why God was asking me to surrender what I thought was best for my baby with what was actually needed: food that would sustain him when my body so clearly couldn't. Giving Patrick a bottle of formula was a much bigger sacrifice for me than all my crazy attempts to breastfeed.

That afternoon, I bought some formula and gave Patrick a bottle. He sucked down that milk, and the rest was history. He ate and ate and then ate some more, and he grew fat and round and happy. I didn't have to take Patrick for weekly weigh-ins anymore, and, though I was sad and even embarrassed about giving him a bottle, I knew the formula was the right thing for all of us.

Still, it was painful to let go of the ideal, of what I thought was best as Patrick's mother. Catholic writer Simcha Fisher says it this way:

As my kids got older . . . I found myself face to face with a whole new kind of sacrifice: sacrificing your idea of what kind of mother I was—my idea of what it *means* to be a mother. . . .

Good parents are the ones who try as hard as they can to do what seems right to them, but still allow themselves to say, "This just isn't working. Let's try something else. . . .

Good parents are the ones who say, "I always thought we'd be THIS kind of family . . . have THIS kind of education . . . spend our time on *these* kind of things with *these* kinds of people . . . but instead, here we are." Here we are, responding to our actual circumstances, taking care of our actual children, leading our actual lives.

Sometimes, we just have to acknowledge that life has its indisputable stinkiness, and that our own stupid choices, or our own stupid fates, have made it impossible to have what is clearly superior. But sometimes, we end up open being grateful for our failures, because it makes one thing really clear: we're not here to be particular kinds of parents. We're here to be the parents of particular kids.[1]

Patrick was in my arms for only ten days before I confronted what Fisher describes and wrestled with what I desired versus what could actually be. Nursing Patrick was not in the cards, and I had to settle on a less-than-perfect alternative.

When Nothing Goes as Planned

When Patrick was about twelve months old, I brought him to our family doctor for a checkup. I was concerned because he had developed some obvious, nickel-sized, carrot colored patches on the top of his scalp. They appeared overnight, and I wondered if the doctor knew what they were. Our pediatrician examined Patrick thoroughly and then quickly excused himself from the room. When he came back he said, "Colleen, Patrick has a few of the markers for a genetic disorder called neurofibromatosis. These patches on his scalp have me concerned. You need to take him to a dermatologist and then to a geneticist. Something else is going on with Patrick's health."

I was stunned. I too was concerned about his development, especially because Patrick was physically delayed, though I never considered a *disorder* might be at the root of the issue.

I had made peace with my struggle to nurse Patrick, yet my acceptance didn't reduce the challenges I faced in feeding him. Patrick struggled to gain weight from the time he was born. He had acute, undiagnosed reflux and vomited up most of his meals. I'd feed him a bottle and then he would project it across the room, all over me, and all over his clothes. I'd clean us up and start again. I spent most of Patrick's first year trying to get that kid to eat and keep his food down. When I introduced solid foods, he couldn't properly chew, so he swallowed things whole instead of using his teeth to break up his meal. I constantly worried he would choke on a grape or piece of chicken because of his unconventional table manners. He also faced physical struggles. At a year old, he wasn't crawling much, and he was almost two before he learned to walk.

I made an appointment with the specialists. The dermatologist biopsied those bumps on Patrick's head, and although they were benign, the lumps were consistent with the genetic disease our pediatrician mentioned and carried an increased risk for certain types of cancer. We brought Patrick to the geneticist, and he confirmed what we'd been told might be the problem: Patrick was one of the lucky one in three thousand to have the genetic disorder Neurofibromatosis, type 1.

Neurofibromatosis (NF) causes tissue along the nerves to grow. This growth can put pressure on affected nerves, causing pain. Most of the time, the skin growths cause no problems. Sometimes, however, the growths develop on nerves, and nerve damage or loss of function in the area affected by the nerve can occur. Some of the symptoms of NF include shortened stature, delayed physical motor development, tumors, learning disability, softening of the bone, curvature of the spine, and an increased risk of cancer. It's also possible for tumors to grow in inopportune spots like the brain, spinal cord, or cranial nerve.

It was a lot of information to digest, although the diagnosis did explain a few things about Patrick, like why he could never nurse properly. Patrick simply wasn't strong enough to draw milk. It also explained his general muscle weakness and his inability to crawl, even at a year old. The little guy simply didn't have the strength he needed to support his own body and move at the same time. While my friends' children emptied cabinets and crawled on top of tables, Patrick sat in the middle of my living room floor, his magnetic smile zapping me with its energy from a mile away, completely unable to move on his own. Any milestone he did meet was with the help of both physical and occupational therapists, who came to our house several times a week for his strength training exercises.

After the shock wore off, the diagnosis provided us some comfort because we now had information. We could come up with a plan to help him thrive or at least meet basic milestones. If something new popped up in his development that was atypical, we could consult a book or a doctor and know what to expect. Plus, the therapy interventions were a huge help in motivating Patrick toward physical mobility. We had a team of people monitoring his development, and we implemented as many of their suggestions at home as we could. Slowly but surely, Patrick began to master basic motor skills, and everyone was thrilled. I became friends with the nurses and the therapists. John and I hated that he had a disorder, but everything we'd read told us most kids with NF lead normal, mostly uncomplicated lives. We anticipated Patrick would have some hurdles to overcome, but we guessed he'd probably be just fine.

We guessed wrong.

My Plan versus Reality

I put Patrick down early for a nap one afternoon, just a few weeks after his third birthday. My mother had arrived from out of town to watch our children. John had planned an overnight trip for the two of us at a bed and breakfast a few hours away, for the first time since we'd been married. My mom, sister, and I were chatting in my living room when I heard Patrick scream. It wasn't a normal cry, and I knew something was wrong, so I darted back to his room and picked him up from his crib.

When I found him, he was limp, unable to walk unassisted, and wailing uncontrollably. Our next-door neighbor, Louis, was an ER doctor, and I was good friends with his wife, Ashley. I threw Patrick in the car and drove over to their house to see if Louis could look at him. I banged on Ashley's door, yelling to her I needed Louis's help. Ashley saw my panicked face when she appeared and called for her husband. Louis had just come in from his nightshift; when he heard Ashley shout to get up, he stumbled out of his bedroom, pulling his pants on as he went so he could look at Patrick. He ran to examine Patrick, who was strapped into his seat in my vehicle. After a minute, he patted Patrick's head and then looked at me in the eyes and said, "I think he's had a seizure. Take him to the ER."

Up to that point, most of Patrick's visits to the doctor had been routine checkups but in an instant, everything changed. When we got to the emergency room, Patrick was admitted and endured an MRI, a cat scan, an EEG, multiple blood draws, and even a spinal tap. Once the medical professionals conducted all their tests and reviewed all the information, which took days, a neurologist entered our room and confirmed Patrick's seizure. An image of Patrick's brain glowed on one of the walls. She pointed to it and said, "The MRI demonstrates an abnormality on Patrick's left parietal lobe. This here, I assume, is causing Patrick's difficulty walking. It might be an infection. I don't think it's a tumor, but I'm not sure. In any case, this likely caused his seizure. I'm going to put him on a round of steroids to reduce a possible infection in his brain, and I want to follow his progress."

The doctor's delivery was so matter of fact, detached even, that I cringed. She was simply doing her job and that was the problem: I resented the way she delivered this turn-our-world-upside-down news like it was routine information. This was *not* routine for us. The scans and seizures and spinal taps might have been common to her in her world, but they certainly weren't the norm in ours.

Sadly, this scene and the many like them immediately became our new normal.

For the next year, Patrick continued to have seizures and the doctors continued to admit him into the hospital in order to determine what might be wrong. Patrick ingested a regular cocktail of medication to prevent the seizures and to reduce brain swelling, none of which worked. We were referred to a variety of specialists and all of them, no matter how renowned or expert, were befuddled by his case, unsure about whether his neurological issues were a complication of NF. Eventually, one of our trusted physicians—the one whose phone number we kept with us at all times—suggested a brain biopsy in order to rule out the worst: cancer, tumors, and the like. We consented to this because we were so desperate for answers, but the biopsy, along with the many other invasive tests ordered after that, proved inconclusive.

Shortly after his first seizure, John and I drove to visit some friends for the baptism of their new baby, our godchild. On the evening of our arrival, Patrick had another seizure and was again admitted into a nearby medical facility. The neurologists on call wanted to run a series of tests, which required many vials of blood. Patrick was wasted with exhaustion and fought the nurse and the doctor away from his little veins. The physician held him down while the nurse wrestled to get the needle in. The entire time Patrick screamed, kicked, and begged for my help, "Mommy, Mommy! No! Make them stop! Pick me up! Help me, Mommy! Please, help me!"

I couldn't make them stop. We needed to know what was wrong with Patrick, and I *was* trying to help him. I had to let the medical staff inflict a small amount of pain on my child so we could know what was going on. I put my head down so no one would see me as I began to sob.

"How did I get here?" I prayed. "Why is this happening? You want me to stand here, Lord, and watch
him suffer? Do you hear his pain? His cry? Is this what
you want? I can't do it."

In my mind, an image of Mother Mary appeared
at the foot of the Cross. I realized she too had watched
her own son's agony and torture and now Jesus was
asking me to do the same. I felt a deep and immediate
sense of peace.[2]

The doctors eventually collected what they needed
and left the room. I scooped Patrick up and rocked him
until they ordered the next round of tests. We spent the
weekend at the hospital, not at the baptism like we'd
originally planned.

When faced with a child's chronic illness, a parental
review of the worst-case scenario is inevitable. For me,
this would usually happen in the middle of the night,
after I was awakened by a crying child and had settled them. Crawling back into my own bed, I dreaded
the next few hours as I knew I would lay awake in a
darkened room, besieged with the terrible thoughts that
could happen:

What if Patrick didn't recover from one of his bad
seizures?

What if the doctors never discovered what was
wrong with him?

What if Patrick died?

Here's an honest confession: I never asked for a
miraculous healing for my son. I begged others to pray,
especially the morning after a sleepless night of worry,
but I never asked Jesus directly to heal my child. What
if he didn't honor my request? I knew my faith was too
weak to withstand Patrick's death so instead, I prayed,
"Lord, I do believe, help my unbelief" (Mk 9:24). This,

of course, is the same prayer uttered by another parent, one in the scriptures, who had also doubted God's ability to perfectly heal. The father brought his possessed son to the disciples first, but when the disciples were unsuccessful in their efforts, the boy's father implored Jesus to help: "But if you can do anything, have compassion on us and help us." Jesus replied, "'If you can?' Everything is possible to one who has faith." At this, the boy's father cried out, "Lord, I do believe, help my unbelief!" (Mk 9:22–24)

Just like the father in the scriptures who had turned to the disciples for help, I had gone to medical professionals—the people who were supposed to know how to heal Patrick—yet they couldn't heal my son. None of the doctors knew what was wrong with Patrick, and I felt as though they hadn't done their jobs. Looking back, this was probably an unfair attitude because many of those doctors loved Patrick, were so kind to my family, and did all they could to help him. Still, they couldn't diagnose what was wrong with him and they couldn't make him better. Consequently, I felt like they failed both Patrick *and* me.

Despair threatened to overtake me, and I had to fight drowning in it. I did have faith God could help us, but my faith that he would actually do so—that he would come to our aid and heal Patrick—was weak. Our situation seemed so hopeless; I needed Jesus to grow my faith, to help me trust him, so I repeatedly prayed "Lord, I do believe, help my unbelief!" The prayer became my battle cry; it was probably the first real prayer I ever uttered.

One of the most painful experiences of that year was the day I found myself in the oncology ward of Texas Children's Hospital. By this time, I was a professional at navigating appointments with specialists, but that morning as I sat in the beautifully decorated waiting room, I felt irritable and annoyed. The bright yellow paint color, the wall of windows that allowed the sunshine to pour in, and the smiley-faced scrubs worn by the nurses irked me instead of making me feel more comfortable. I was distressed about a visit to the cancer doctor and yellow paint and smiley-faced nursing scrubs wouldn't change that, though I couldn't fault the office staff for trying.

The waiting room was busy, filled with patients—new and old—waiting to see cancer specialists. Patrick and I sat a long time, hoping a nurse would call us back. I tried to entertain him and distract him, but it was a difficult feat. I was emotionally overwrought and longed to sleep, but that was an impossible proposition because Patrick wanted me to read to him and watch him build Duplos at the table provided for the kids.

Finally, after several hours, a nurse called us back to another waiting room. We settled ourselves in a new waiting room, cautiously optimistic that we might set eyes on our doctor soon, when I noticed a little girl positioned directly across from me. She sat in a wheelchair while an IV dripped into her veins. She wore a pretty silk scarf over her bald head. I didn't want to stare, so I forced myself to look at the floor. Tears burned my eyes, and I sternly issued silent warnings to myself: *Do not cry. Do not start crying. Pull yourself together.* When an image of Patrick sitting in the little girl's spot appeared before my eyes, I thought I might audibly sob. I blinked the thought away and continued with the self-talk, coaching myself over and over to stave off my emotional breakdown.

We waited for several more hours until the nurse encouraged us to go to the hospital cafeteria for lunch. I was starved, so I grabbed Patrick's hand and we made our way to the food court. There, we discovered every fast food option known to mankind. I was on emotional overload, and the brief reprieve from the oncology ward forced me into the fleeting, comforting arms of food, including three gigantic soft cookies. I had barely finished my meal when I realized I had overeaten and felt sick.

When we arrived back at the office, the nurse immediately called us into a room and we met the doctor. I handed him all of Patrick's medical information—which filled an entire binder—and he examined Patrick. The man was gentle with Patrick, kind and joking, and when he was finished, he turned to look at me.

"How are *you* doing?" he asked.

Before I could stop myself, I blurted out, "I just spent the last fifty minutes stuffing my face. I feel like I'm gonna throw up."

The doctor nodded his head up and down, understanding permeating his face. "You know, I'm an oncologist. I hate cigarettes, but sometimes I go downstairs and I see parents smoking outside and I think, *They've got a really sick kid in there. I'd probably smoke too.* I try not to be too hard on them. Don't worry too much about the cookies."

In my entire life, I don't think I've ever felt so consoled.

"And I think for now," he said, "we can rule out cancer for little Patrick."

When the appointment was over, Patrick and I gathered our stuff and went to the elevator. I pushed the down button, and while we waited for the sound to signal the opening doors, I blinked back tears for the twentieth time that day. I was grateful Patrick didn't have cancer, relieved he wouldn't have to endure the treatments like that little girl in the waiting room, but I was still worried about my very sick child. It would be another six more months of medical testing and hospital stays before we learned a special diet was the key to keeping Patrick seizure free. Once we implemented the diet, the seizures stopped and his health dramatically improved.[3]

What Patrick's Illness Taught Me

When I first became a parent, I thought my biggest challenge would involve deciding which language Patrick would master first—French or Spanish? I figured he and I would spend most days reading children's literature, and at night John and I would research schools with elite academic reputations. I intended to teach him to read early and memorize all the state capitols and US presidents. I planned on only the best nutrition—my mother's milk and organic foods. Instead, I spent those first few years with him panicked about his weight, poor diet, and inability to keep down food. I drove back and forth from therapy appointments multiple times a week, and when we arrived home I spent time setting up obstacle courses in the living room to encourage Patrick to move. We expended so much time, energy, and money teaching Patrick basic skills like eating, crawling, and walking—skills my other friends' children performed without thinking about them—I had no time or desire to attempt lofty ones like early reading goals or memorization of math facts. I quickly learned *never* to wish away any developmental milestone for any of my children and to be thankful for every small accomplishment. Any progress Patrick attained was hard won, a Herculean feat mastered by a tiny boy.

Before I actually had children, I believed one of my most important jobs would be to give them the best, academically and socially. Outside of our Catholic faith, those were the areas I would expend my greatest effort and energy, or at least, that's what I thought. But a lot of the stuff I considered important prior to Patrick's diagnosis fell into the nonessential category after. Prep schools, academic success, and athleticism were no longer a priority for me; Patrick's knowledge and love of Jesus was of dire consequence. Patrick's illness was an invitation to surrender what I thought I wanted—multilingual kids with the intellectual rigor of Thomas Aquinas—and replace it with what was most important—kids who wanted to become saints. Worldly success wasn't at the top of my to-do list anymore, and neither were the "perfect" children I initially coveted, mainly because Patrick didn't fit in my definition of "perfect." The fact that Patrick couldn't do certain things didn't change our love for him. He wasn't perfect, but he was perfect for our family.

Still, his illness affected our lives. I never could have predicted what a year-long medical saga filled with hospital stays, bills, and invasive medical tests would look like, and there was no way of knowing how it would *feel*. I thought he and I would spend afternoons at the park, not working with multiple therapists in our home multiple times a week. If was far from what I had planned for us, and it made me reflect not only about my priorities, but also about what would happen if Patrick died. The idea was so painful it could knock the wind right out of me, though it had to be considered given the circumstances.

I had one conviction and profound consolation that kept my head floating above deep waters of sadness during this time: if Patrick died, he would become a saint. He was not at the age of reason and there was no sin on his soul. His purpose here on earth would be complete, and he would be united with Jesus in heaven. Patrick would have fought the good fight, and he would have won the race. I would have done my job as a Catholic parent: I would have supported Patrick through his illness as best I could, offering him the best medical and therapeutic interventions within my means, and Patrick would actually have become perfect, just not the way I had originally intended.

Patrick's illness taught me I don't need to create a game plan for success for my kids because God already has that covered. His plan sometimes involves using challenges I might not have selected, yet the challenges are surefire ways for them to encounter Christ, as long as they stay open to him. It's painful, as mothers, to watch our children suffer, but their suffering is never in vain, especially if it unites them with Jesus.

Patrick, thankfully, didn't die. God saw fit to answer the many prayers offered on his behalf. Patrick's health significantly improved, but he does still face certain challenges my other children don't. Although he's fourteen years old now, Patrick is much smaller than his peers. He maintains a pretty strict diet, which sets him apart from the other children. He is chronically underweight, and he gets frustrated because no matter what he does, his growth is almost nonexistent. We have to keep a close eye on his health, meeting regularly with specialists for checkups.

But Patrick has many gifts.

He's smart and loves school, despite warnings that he would have learning troubles and would need educational interventions. He spends his free time writing stories and reading history books. His dream in life is to be a military history professor who flies airplanes. He can't decide if he should be a priest because he's afraid he won't be able to teach at the college level. He has many natural gifts and abilities, but he can never quite forget about his disease. It reminds him of his weakness, his dependence on God. It keeps his eyes focused on Jesus, not on his own amazing abilities.

Patrick's suffering is one of the instruments God will use to perfect Patrick, if he allows it. Just as the father ran to meet the prodigal son who returned home after living a life of sinful indulgence, the Lord will meet our children on the road in which they suffer. He will make them holy on that road, even if it's a road we never wanted them to go down in the first place.

God Can Use Anything to Bring Us into His Love

By the end of his high school career, my brother was an alcoholic and drug user. When he was twelve, he began smoking cigarettes and drinking beer; by the time he was thirty, he took a plethora of multicolored pills daily. Toward the end of his addiction, and is the case with most users and alcoholics, it was either drugs or death. He chose life, though he admits that without my parents' tough love, he wouldn't be alive today.

Addiction is predictable and cyclical: there's pain, then there's the use of an addictive agent, then comes pain relief, then there are relational consequences, then guilt and shame.[4] Ryan's addictions followed this textbook pattern. What started as a beer here and there with the purpose of attaining a buzz ended, for Ryan, with loneliness, alienation, homelessness, and poverty.

Our parents, after many years, accepted that Ryan's situation wasn't getting any better. It took even longer for them to admit they had been inadvertently helping him continue in a lifestyle they didn't support by giving him a place to stay or money when he needed it. Together, they consulted a therapist and formulated a tough-love plan: he wasn't allowed to move back home again. He couldn't borrow money. They couldn't pick up the tab for pizzas or cell phone bills or car payments. But the pièce de résistance was this: if he came into the house uninvited, they were to call the police. He was no longer welcome at any time.

They phoned him one night to let him know the new rules. He was living with another drug addict, and he laughed at the news.

"I'm serious, Ryan. It's over," Mom said. "We put in an alarm system and you need a code to deactivate it. If it goes off, the system automatically calls the police. Don't come here."

"OK, Mom, I got it. You don't want me at the house," he said.

He was blowing her off, and she knew it. Ryan really hadn't heard anything anyone said for a long time.

It happened one night while my dad was out of town and my mother was on her way home from work. My brother, newly homeless again, showed up on the front door to find the house empty. A master of creative problem solving, Ryan shimmied his way in, activating the newly installed alarm system.

"Hey, Ma, we've got a situation here," he said when he had my mother on the phone. "I'm at the house, and I can't get the alarm to stop beeping. What's the code?"

"Ryan, you're not supposed to be in the house. We told you that. You need to get out now. The police will show in five minutes, and I can't protect you if you are there," she said.

"Ma, come on. Don't be ridiculous. Just give me the code so I can shut off the alarm. I need to crash here tonight."

"You can't, Ryan. You're not allowed. Your father and I told you that already. Leave now or the police will arrest you," she said. He laughed and asked for the code again. He still wasn't listening. Worse, he thought our mother was joking.

"Please, Ryan, leave," she said before hanging up the phone. Tears welled as she realized what she was going to have to do.

A few minutes later, the phone rang. When she answered, she heard laughter in the background. Ryan's smooth-talking had finagled the cop.

"Just give me a sec, officer, we'll clear this right up."

"Ma, I need you to tell the officer I live here. Can you do that for me, Mom?" Ryan said and handed the phone to the man in uniform.

The police officer was annoyed. "Hello," he said, tone brusque. "What's the deal, Mrs. Murphy?"

"Officer, the deal is my son has a drug problem and isn't allowed in our house," she said, choking down a sob.

The officer was silent. He'd just been played, and he knew it.

"You want me to take him, ma'am?" he said, his voice gentler, more apologetic. My mother was silent for a minute.

Do I want my son carted off to jail because he has a drug problem? No, officer, I don't. Do I want to bar my son from my house because he has a drug problem? No, officer, I don't, she thought.

Then she had another thought: *I don't want to watch him die, either. And I don't want to help him do it.*

"You have to take him," she answered the policeman and hung up.

She pulled over her car and sobbed into her steering wheel. Ryan spent the night in jail, and when he was released, he came home. With my dad still out of town, my mother didn't have the resolve to let Ryan sleep on the streets. She let him stay at the house under the condition he get sober and get into a program. She had his attention.

Ryan detoxed, a wicked experience that will motivate the worst addict to stay clean, on our parent's couch. During his time at home, my mother put Ryan in touch with Paul—an old friend of Ryan's who'd used drugs with him in high school. After committing a felony and having a child out of wedlock, Paul had found sobriety in Alcoholics Anonymous; somehow my mom tracked him down and asked him to call Ryan. Paul obliged, and for the next several months, he picked Ryan up and brought him to AA meetings a couple of times a day. He helped find Ryan a place to stay and later helped Ryan acquire a good job. Ryan, through the grace of God, his hard work, and the support of AA, has been clean and sober for almost a decade.

On his first birthday, the term AA uses for celebrating a person's anniversary of their first day of sobriety, our entire family gathered for dinner at a Washington, DC, steakhouse. My parents, my two younger sisters, my husband, and I were present. Ryan's closest AA friends were there, including a man instrumental in his sobriety: his sponsor, William.

After dinner, we attended an AA meeting where a few people shared their stories. My family sat together, front and center, celebrating the lost family member who had been found. When he stood to speak, Ryan choked on his words: "I'm Ryan, and I'm an alcoholic. I've been sober for one year today, and the reason for that is because of the people in this room. My family is sitting in the first row; they are what unconditional love looks like. They told me no when I wasn't ready to hear it. They called the cops on me. They saved my life."

There wasn't a dry eye in the room.

If you asked my mother if drugs and alcohol were the avenue she would have chosen for Ryan to find God, she would have suggested a different path, I'm sure. Watching her son's descent into a quagmire of addiction wasn't what she'd hoped for him; it wasn't what she'd hoped for her family. My mother also knows, however, the Lord found Ryan on the road of suffering. Suffering prompted Ryan to turn his will and his life over to God and away from the idol of drugs and alcohol. The road was long and painful, and my mother had to sit and watch Ryan go down it, despite her warnings and admonishments to him to get off that particular path. It's not natural for any parent to silently observe a suffering child without trying to help, regardless if the pain endured comes from a physical or a moral wound. As mothers and fathers, we tend, we nurse, and we make things better. We don't just sit and watch.

Yet that is just what Mary did. When the angel Gabriel appeared to ask Mary to carry the Savior of the world, Mary must have known her inexplicable predicament might scare Joseph away, yet she trusted God with the outcome. Despite not wanting to lose Joseph, she endured a period of time when she didn't know for sure what was going to happen. She didn't threaten or cajole Joseph. She simply sat and watched and waited.

After an angel appeared to him one night in his dream, Joseph decided to wed Mary. Their son, Jesus, was born a short time later in a humble stable to parents without an impressive family history and with no money. Eight days after the birth of Jesus, Mary and Joseph, like the observant Jews they were, brought their baby to the temple to present him, where Simeon predicted that a sword of sorrow would pierce Mary's heart. Mary had just given birth to the Savior of the world; she was probably in the highest echelon of new-mom bliss when a stranger said to her, "This baby is precious, but he's going to be the cause of some intense personal suffering." That forewarning would be hard to swallow for *any* mom, but Mary also happened to be the Mother of God. I imagine her desire to protect him would have been more than a little intense. Worse still, Mary didn't know what kind of suffering Simeon was alluding to. If she indulged any daydreams for even a little bit, she probably could have come up with some pretty elaborate, horrible scenarios. Instead, Mother Mary again surrendered her desire to control and protect her son and entrusted his future to God. For many years, Mary sat and watched and waited for this suffering to manifest itself.

The suffering, of course, came during Jesus' three-year public ministry. The *Catechism* states, "Certain Pharisees and partisans of Herod together with priests and scribes agreed together to destroy Jesus. . . . He is accused of blasphemy and false prophecy, religious crimes which the Law punished with death by stoning" (*CCC*, 574). Jesus' mother, Mary, watched every moment of his demise. I have trouble restraining myself when

I see a kid being rude to my child on the playground, yet Mother Mary sat *silently* and watched as her son endured the beatings of the worst kind of bullies.

Mary was present at Jesus' scourging at the pillar where soldiers hit him so brutally his flesh ripped off his body. Mary saw the soldiers crown her son with thorns so sharp, his scalp and forehead were pierced and blood flowed out. Mary watched as her son carried a Cross too heavy for a healthy, strapping man, let alone someone beaten within an inch of his life. And Mary was there, weeping at the foot of the Cross, when her son was crucified. How did she allow people to persecute her innocent child? How did she restrain herself from admonishing Jesus to quit doing God's will? We don't ever hear her complaining about her son's work, nor do we hear her encourage Jesus to abandon it. She doesn't tell Jesus to get down from the Cross and save himself, the way any mother might be tempted to do.

Her son was the victim of abuse, slander, and eventually murder. Despite the injustice, she didn't meddle in his affairs. While Jesus was being nailed to the Cross, she didn't push her way through the crowds yelling, "Take me instead!" Nowhere in the gospels does Mary tell a Pharisee, "You can't talk to my son that way!" Suffering silently, she sat and watched.[5]

Mary saw past the immediate suffering of her son and focused on what was to come—the impending Resurrection, the fact Jesus would save all of us from sin. Mary endured the personal discomfort of Jesus' public ministry and, as a result, shared in Jesus' work of redemption. Francis Xavier Nguyen Van Thuan once wrote, "During the most glorious events of our Lord's public life—his transfiguration on Mount Tabor and his entry into Jerusalem—Mary remained hidden. But at the times of gravest danger—the flight into Egypt, the way of the cross to Calvary, her sorrowful watch at the foot of the cross, and her vigil in the upper room with the apostles—Mary courageously chose to be present. She did not live for herself, but only for the Lord and His work of redemption."[6]

Is it painful for you to sit and watch as your children suffer? Are you burdened by poverty or grave illness or familial addiction and generational sin? Are you pained by your grown child's lapse of faith?

Run to Mother Mary, "the consoler of the afflicted," "help of Christians," and "the refuge of sinners."[7] "She has crushed the head of the serpent. She will help you to conquer the devil, 'the flesh,' and 'the world.' She will obtain for you the graces to hold firm to the noble ideal, which the Lord has placed in your heart." "No matter how tepid, sinful or hopeless you may feel, entrust yourself into the hands of Mary. Jesus bequeathed her to you; how could she abandon you?"[8]

Mother Mary knows firsthand the difficulties you face in parenting your children, in watching and waiting as they suffer. She knows how painful it is to surrender to God the moral and physical wounds our children face, and she will not abandon us, even if the situation seems bleak and beyond repair. Mary is our model and our friend for enduring the pressure cooker we sometimes experience in family life, and we can have confidence that she will not leave us to endure the pain alone. Mary sat and watched and waited while her own son suffered, and she watches and waits with us as we suffer too.

Another Mom Who Watched

Mother Mary is not the only Catholic mother who endured the painful experiences of a grown child. St. Monica, mother of the great Doctor of the Church St. Augustine, also had to stand by as her son sank into lust and heresy before settling into the truths held in the Catholic Church. Even as a schoolboy, Augustine was a difficult child who misbehaved and lied about his schoolwork even though he was gifted intellectually. As a teenager, he developed unhealthy friendships and engaged in rebellious activity, even stealing because he derived pleasure from the forbidden nature of the act. As an adult, he cohabitated with a woman and together they had a child out of wedlock, though Augustine had no intention of ever marrying the woman. Augustine's choices were devastating to his mother, a devout Christian who prayed that her son would know and love God. Monica watched her son's moral demise, mourned the choices her son made, entreated him to come to his senses, and begged God to protect his soul.[9]

But she couldn't get him to do the right thing.

Unlike Mother Mary, Monica was not detached as she observed her son's affairs. In fact, she may have been the world's first helicopter mom. Monica persevered when she needed to back off; she interjected when she needed to stay silent; she followed Augustine when she needed to detach. However, the one thing she did not ever do was quit praying for her son's soul. In *The Confessions*, St. Augustine writes, "You sent Your hand from above, and drew my soul out of that profound darkness, when my mother, Your faithful one, wept to You on my behalf more than mothers are wont to weep the bodily death of their children. For she saw that I was dead by that faith and spirit which she had from You, and You heard her, O Lord. You heard her, and despised not her tears, when, pouring down, they watered the earth under her eyes in every place where she prayed; yea, You heard her."[10]

Augustine credits these prayers Monica offered on his behalf as she sat and watched his moral demise as the key component in saving him. Monica eventually learned to surrender her self-reliant tendencies and instead asked God to do what she couldn't: heal her son. Monica turned to God in her deep suffering and entrusted to him the saving work of Augustine. Her prayers eventually converted her wayward boy, and he became one of the greatest theologians in the history of the Catholic Church. Monica herself was unable to heal Augustine, but she trusted in God's healing powers, and he came to the rescue.

For a long time, however, Monica too had to sit and watch as her boy suffered. Mary couldn't choose Jesus' anguish, and Monica couldn't choose Augustine's, just like I had no say in Patrick's suffering and my mom had no voice in my brother's. The only recourse a parent has in these situations is to embrace the belief that silent prayers and faithful example will be good enough to convert those we love. Although all parents want to protect their children, often they must trust God to handle the situation. Instead of "fixing," we are often called to sit and watch and wait for God.

He will not abandon us.

Closing Prayer

Lord, one of the most painful experiences in my life has been watching as my children suffer. Their pain makes me want to control and manipulate instead of leaning into you. Remove from me the high burden of responsibility I feel to fix life or to escape pain, especially when times are hardest. I trust you have given me the strength to bear my burdens and those of my children with grace.

When I am uncertain about my children's futures, reassure me of your presence. I know you have not abandoned us but that you are with us and you want, even more than I do, to be united with my children in eternity. Keep them close to you, Lord. I trust your plan for my children is even better than I could imagine, and I surrender all my hopes, dreams, and desires for them to you. Amen.

Discussion Questions

1. What is the greatest suffering you've experienced as a parent? Was God able to draw good from this suffering? If so, how and in what ways?
2. Do you try to avoid suffering? Why?
3. When you experience your child's suffering, how do you react? What are some healthy ways you could detach yet still show love and compassion to the suffering child?
4. Do you believe suffering can be redemptive? How have you suffered as a parent? What can Mother Mary teach us?
5. Romans 8:28 states, "We know that all things work for good for those who love God, who are called according to his purpose." Do you believe God is in charge and directing things according to his plan?

Confession 5

I SOMETIMES COMPARE MYSELF WITH OTHER PARENTS

How much trouble he avoids who does not look to see what others say or do, but only what he does himself, that it may be just and pure.
—Marcus Arelius, *Meditations*

I hosted our weekly playgroup for moms and children one Friday morning about a year before Patrick got sick. After I had separated two ragamuffins for fighting over some toy and before I helped myself to a second donut, the conversation turned to Gymboree classes. I was Gymboree clueless, but my friends' passionate discussion of vinyl, primary-colored play mats, wall mirrors, and teacher-led songs and games piqued my interest. I thought the use of ball pits and indoor play centers for delirious kids to empty an infinite amount of energy was pure ingenuity. The longer I heard the other parents boast the benefits of developing physical dexterity and prowess early, the more I *knew* Gymboree was designed for us.

That afternoon, after I said goodbye to the last family and swept the last stray Cheerios into the trash, I hightailed it to my computer. I scoured the Internet looking for prices and available classes. My research confirmed what I suspected: Gymboree was way out of our league. John and I were young and poor, and there was no money for this kind of thing.

Still, if my children were to have a fighting chance at life, I knew Gymboree was necessary. So I did what I've done since the very first day I became a parent: I hit the panic button. The bell sounded, reverberating deep within my very being, and I responded in my typical, neurotic way with the question that would fuel my worry until the next panic alarm: *How can I bring Gymboree classes from Duggan-dream to Duggan-reality?*

I met John at the front door that evening and gave him a minute to unwind before I casually brought up my concern.

"John," I said. "All"—read: approximately two out of ten—"of the playgroup moms have enrolled their kids in Gymboree classes."

John looked confused.

"What's Gymboree?" he asked.

I charitably took it upon myself to instruct the ignorant. I emphasized the use of classical songs—brilliant compositions of music such as "How Much Is That Doggy in the Window?" and "Do You Know the Muffin Man?"—to develop pitch, tone, and melody in children. I also mentioned how the complex architecture—multipieced vinyl soft gym sets made of foam—enhanced physical development. I finished my sales pitch, and he gave me a blank look.

"And why do the kids need this?"

"Are you serious?" I said, "What if Meaghan is the next Nadia Comaneci and she never realizes it because she didn't have Gymboree? We will be responsible, John. You and me! Her parents! The people given to her by God to help her realize her innate gifts. Do you want that on your conscience? Do you want to tell God, 'I'm sorry, we blew it with Meaghan because we were too poor for Gymboree classes'?"

John shrugged his shoulders. Clearly, he wasn't as concerned as I.

"We need to figure out a way for the kids to participate," I said. "It's what good parents do; they put their kids in Gymboree."

"Colleen," he said, "I think the kids will be OK, even without Gymboree."

"Do you know what's out there, John? Drugs. Gangs. Prostitution. Gymboree will keep them busy."

"Patrick is two and Meaghan is one," he said.

"What does that have to do with anything?" I yelled. "Gymboree is our duty."

I think at that point, John walked away. His interest in my mounting neurosis was nonexistent. I shouted one final jab as he walked down the hall: "Don't blame me when Meaghan comes to you crying one day because she's not Mary Lou Retton."

In the end, John was right. Patrick, Meaghan, and our four other children have all survived without Gymboree. It only took me ten years to realize Gymboree, like so many other "necessary" activities for children, is more for the parents than the kids.

I didn't know it then, but that early concern my kids would fail at life because we didn't provide Gymboree lessons was just the tip of the parental iceberg of extra-curricular worries. Since then, there have been many other times I compared what we could offer our children with what another family offered theirs. I still sometimes catch myself wondering, *Am I giving them the very best? Shouldn't all children have the chance to attend rocket camp or go on a mission trip through the south of France or*

*participate in an international children's choir that performs
at Carnegie Hall?*

These just seem like good, worthwhile opportunities, right? Why *wouldn't* I want these things for my
kids?

What complicates the desire to offer beneficial
opportunities to our children is that it's become a cultural norm for parents to enroll children in as many
activities as possible. It's what good parents *do*. The
pressure to keep up with the Jones's kids is ever-pres-
ent and real.

Moms and dads tote kids from music lessons to
dance classes to robotics clubs to sports practices, doing
whatever it takes to make sure their children have a
"successful" life, even using credit cards or mortgaging
the house to pay for extracurriculars. More opportunities mean more chances for success in life, these parents
reason. Family life revolves then around outside commitments instead of around nurturing relationships.[1]

I'm sympathetic to the plight of parents who, with
the best of intentions, want to give their children all they
can and who nudge, or bulldoze, their children to excel.
I'd be lying if I said I didn't want my children to have
what it takes to succeed.

But when did a frazzled home life in the name of
excellent education and extracurricular activities become
the acceptable standard? And are these things what our
children really need? One of the great gifts of Patrick's
illness was that I saw very clearly that the most important task in my parental job description was to love, support, and be present to him; it was not to make sure he
attended Gymboree five times a week (nothing against
Gymboree). When he had a medical test, I was supposed
to hold his hand and whisper love into his ear. When he

performed a hard task in physical therapy, I was supposed to stand on the sideline, watch him struggle, and then shout "Attaboy!" and "You can do it!"

And now that Patrick is no longer life-threateningly ill? Nothing much has changed. Patrick and all my children still mainly need my love, my attention, and my support. They want me to love their father and fight for a good marriage. In the short term, they may think they *need* ballet classes and track-and-field and straight A's without studying. They might also think it's my job to provide them those things. But Patrick's illness affirmed for me that the pomp and the circumstance is not what they *really* require. What my kids really need is a sane, attentive, fully present mom; a peaceful home; and parents who love each other. They need me to tell them they have what it takes to survive in this world. What they don't need is an overbearing mother pushing them to excel in school and sports and making herself crazy in the process.

Don't misunderstand: I'm not against extracurricular activities or good education. I care about my children's worldly future and devote my time to supporting them in their various endeavors. I am against, however, what ridiculous academic pressures and extracurricular activities do to families. I'm against a world where families don't eat together or throw the football outside or read books together. I'm against a schedule so packed with activities that children can't foster creativity or catch frogs in the pond because they are so stressed out over school and sports. I'm against a marriage that can't survive amid the children's schedules. I'm against stressed-out parents who can't come up for air because they are burdened by their children's schedules.

In a perfect world, where I possessed endless energy, resources, and opportunities, I might enroll all my children in activities naturally suited for each of them, no matter the cost—emotionally, financially, temporally, or otherwise.

But not if it killed our family life, and not if it killed me.

The reality is, our family size, limited resources, and parenting abilities prevent certain activities John and I both think are beneficial and wholesome. Over the years, I've had to accept that just because an activity is beneficial for some children does not mean it is beneficial for our children. For instance, when Patrick was in fourth grade, our family dropped out of Boy Scouts. We simply couldn't figure out how to keep up with badges, meetings, and camping trips *and* maintain familial sanity. We loved the families who participated, we found the skills the boys learned truly valuable, and we approved of the many bonding opportunities the boys shared. We couldn't hack the commitment, though.

I wondered how other families made it happen, many of them in a similar state of life as us. Eventually, I realized it didn't matter why or how another family continued to participate; what mattered was that participation in the program created a problem within *our* family life. Ignoring those problems led to strains and resulted in an even more chaotic household. I had to be honest about those limitations and not compare my family and myself to others. What other families decided didn't really matter; what counted was what we felt called to do, and peace in our household, along with nurturing positive relationships, is a priority for us. The Boy Scouts became an obstacle to that familial goal, so we quit.

I want my family to stay out of the rat race and maintain focus on what's important—discerning and doing God's will—which means we protect our time and are careful about any extra commitments. We support our children if they demonstrate a proclivity in a certain area, but we don't worry we won't discover their gifts unless they are enrolled in every single activity out there. If God gave them a talent, do I really believe he will fail to reveal it to them?

Compare Then Despair

In those early years of parenting, though, I spent a fair amount of time worrying about the future well-being of my offspring, and I felt like a failure if I wasn't providing an activity or implementing a family practice that seemed wholesome and good. This distress was magnified exponentially, however, when I compared my efforts to raise my children in the Catholic faith against those of another family who forged a different, but also thoroughly Catholic, path. It was one thing to worry about my child's placement on the best soccer team, but what about our duty to raise Catholic kids? We were committed to Catholic instruction—teaching our kids to pray and exposing them to the sacraments—but what if the way we did it was different from another family's method? What if the path we chose was not as good?

When I looked around, there were many people who seemed to have the market cornered on how to be a good Catholic parent. I noticed the father with eight children file into the pew for daily Mass while we only had two children and wondered, *What's wrong with me that I can't manage my two little ones at Mass? Will my children be heathens, doomed to failure because of their deadbeat Catholic mom?* I saw a veiled woman followed by her sea of children in matching lace, and I wondered, *Should I be doing that too? Am I doing enough to encourage reverence and piety in my children?* I saw others make the decision to adopt a particular method of education, and I agonized about whether our educational decisions for our children were the right ones. I saw the parents who produced not one but two religious vocations within the same family, and I wondered how they attained those results. I saw the great trust some families placed in God's providence when they welcomed another child, and I compared my struggles taking care of three children against their calm confidence. I thought, *I'm drowning with the three kids we've got; would we be OK if we added another? Am I generous enough?*

Maybe these comparisons don't resonate with you—maybe you've compared yourself against the two-parent family that dutifully brings their children to Mass each week while you sit alone mourning the loss of your spouse. Maybe you struggle with the married couple who can't keep their hands off each other because they are still so in love after all these years, or the woman at your church who just had a baby and walked out of the hospital wearing skinny jeans, or the devout, high-powered Catholic dad who makes lots of money and manages the family Rosary every night. The point is, we all have our Achilles' heels when it comes to comparing; we've all looked at another parent and wondered, *How do they do it and should I be doing that too?*

The Fraudulent Catholic Parent?

Many years ago, I attended a Catholic convention. I was wandering around an auditorium piled high with enough books to fill a football stadium when I bumped into an acquaintance from church. We exchanged a hug and general pleasantries and then my friend leaned into me and whispered, "My family doesn't belong here."

I grabbed her hand and said, "Of course they do!"

The woman shook her head and insisted her entrance into this Catholic club had all been some kind of mistake; she and her family were frauds, and they didn't belong. I didn't know how to convince her otherwise. She was comparing her insides with the outsides of the Catholics around her. Even though *all* families have their issues or bad behaviors that need to be improved upon, she was convinced her family was the worst, the least holy of these. She thought her family was beyond help, especially when she compared them against the other "holier"-looking families.

I could relate. How many times had I had a weak moment and yelled at my child only to think, "If [insert the name of my Catholic friend] knew what a bad parent I was, they would insist I turn in my Catholic card."

How many times had my husband and I had a passionate argument on the way to church of all places, and how many times had I slunk into a pew worried I was nothing but a whitewashed tomb with no hope for a thriving marriage? How many times had I compared myself to the other, holier, more peaceful and definitely more functional (at least in my mind) families sitting next to me? How many times had I listened to another parent, full of bravado as they regaled me with their parental platitudes, and been overwhelmed with my own lack of certainty? How many times had I walked away from that parent feeling like God had made a big mistake in giving me this enormous responsibility of child-rearing?

How many times had I, in the quiet hours of the early morning, questioned my Catholic parenting methods, obsessed over my failures and weaknesses and sins?

How many times had I been defensive and over-sensitive when someone questioned my methods or approach?

I could identify with my friend's sentiments at the convention because I knew what life was like behind the closed doors of our home and that it had to be worse than what was behind my friends' doors. It certainly *felt* worse in the explosive moments that sometimes happen in family life. For years, not only did I feel like I was failing at Catholic parenting but I felt like our family dysfunction kept us at arm's length from all the better, holier Catholics. I was so aware of my imperfections and those of my family members that I felt separate from the other Catholic parents in the trenches who were like me, just trying to do the best they could.

I also experienced a real lack of honesty and empathy within Catholic circles about the challenges that sprout up in family life. I can't count the number of times I've tried to commiserate with another good Catholic about the challenges I encountered in marriage or parenting and have been met with wide eyes, silence, judgment, or worse, unsolicited advice.

One morning a few years back, the kids and I had to be somewhere early. I was racing around looking for missing shoes, packing snacks, making sure no one had obvious stains on their clothing, and yelling for all the children to "Get in the *car*! Move, move, move!" I could tell my frantic disposition had been absorbed by our three-year-old because, when I grabbed his hand to guide him into the car, he said, "Damn it, damn it, damn it, damn it!" down each of our porch steps.

It was not a stellar parenting moment, both horri-fying and hilarious at the same time. That afternoon, I still felt uneasy from our chaotic morning and wanted another adult to empathize with me, to tell me I wasn't alone in this crazy crapshoot known as parenting. I was at an event with some other seasoned Catholics, so I decided to bring some levity to the conversation by showcasing the story of my son's new lexicon. Perhaps I was too flippant in my retelling of what happened or perhaps I came off as if it didn't really matter my child was using curse words, but the truth was I felt like a complete failure. I hated the way I had conducted myself that morning, and I felt even worse when the toddler started repeating words he learned from me. I wanted to feel consoled with the knowledge other parents made mistakes too.

In a misguided attempt to feel normal, I relayed the tale of our morning. As I finished, one of the parents looked at me and said, "You really need to work on that, Colleen."

I felt as if someone punched me in the gut.

Yes, it's true: I needed to rectify my habit of cursing in front of the toddlers, but obviously, I already *knew* that. What I wanted in that moment was for another per-son to say, "I've been there. We've all been there. You're human. You make mistakes. Everything is going to be OK." Instead, I felt more shame and embarrassment.

Almost every parent I know has been humbled at least one time by the questionable behavior of a child, behavior the child may have learned from the parent. It's impossible to handle every moment with our chil-dren perfectly. Unfortunately, within Catholic parenting circles, I often found a lack of honesty about these strug-gles, as well as a lack of sense of humor.

One of the most painful examples of unsolicited advice I ever received from another Catholic parent came just a few short months after I began giving Patrick a bottle. He was about six months old, and a few friends and I attended a Catholic conference. I woke up early one morning, packed a trunkful of unnecessary baby gear into the vehicle to take with me, kissed John goodbye, and made my way to the airport with Patrick as my travel companion. I was excited to eat good food, be spiritually nourished, and spend time with my closest friends in a swanky hotel for the weekend. Together, we shared baby strollers and diaper bags and roared with laughter deep into the night. I was having such a good time listening to the lectures and visiting with my girlfriends, I was caught off guard when another woman approached me between one of the sessions and said, "You know, if you really wanted to breastfeed your baby, you could. There are ways to do it. You don't have to give him a bottle if you don't want to."

"I know," I said as I choked back tears. I turned my back on her because I didn't want her to see me cry, and I walked away.

I believe the stranger at the conference meant well, but she assumed a lot when she approached me. She assumed Patrick was my biological child. She assumed he was in perfect health and able to nurse. She assumed I hadn't tried all of the available options out there to help a mother continue to breastfeed. She assumed breastfeeding a child is always the right way. While most parents and doctors would agree breastfeeding is typically best for both mother and baby, if there was one thing Patrick had already taught me it was that the parenting practices we sometimes covet don't always work out in reality as the best option for all involved. The stranger's unsolicited advice wasn't helpful—her words hurt me.

Catholic parents have to be careful not to moralize parenting preferences. Often well-intentioned parents become so inclined toward a specific approach (dietary choices, natural childbirth, private or home education, family size, stay-at-home parenting—the list goes on forever) their preferences become viewed as a non-negotiable aspect of raising Catholic kids in the Catholic faith. Non-moral parenting preferences then become prerequisites for Catholic parenting. Although certain approaches might nicely correlate with our religious convictions (for example, the similarity between nursing an infant and the sacrifice of the Eucharist), much of what we implement as parents are lifestyle choices, not necessarily Church-approved parenting methods guaranteed to produce practicing Catholics. God gives us a great deal of freedom to make the best decisions for our families based on reason and our resources. There is not a one-size-fits-all approach to raising kids in the Catholic faith. If there were, I would have found it already because I've looked. Unless asked for our opinions, we should refrain from suggesting anything to anyone, especially if the issue is not a matter of faith and morals, and instead we should apply ourselves to our own work. The methods we discern as best for our own families are not necessarily best for all families, but we can have confidence they are probably good enough for our own.

God calls all families to love, follow, and serve him, but the way in which he calls us to do it looks different for everyone. We all need to try our best, assume everyone is doing the same, and recognize the rest is up to God.

Elizabeth Foss explains what happens when we make subjective parenting propensities mandatory for all. She writes:

> We eat our own. We make up litmus tests and then level judgments. Does she dress the way a Christian woman should? Does she wear her hair the way a Christian woman should? Does she go to the "right" parish? Does she manage her finances the "right" way? Use the "right" curriculum? Spend her time the "right" way? Does she have enough children and are they spaced the "right" way? If the answers don't fit what we've decided—in our opinions—constitute holiness, we chew the woman up and spit her out in disgust.
>
> And we become women of opinion, not conviction, to use a phrase coined by Colleen Mitchell. We become women who are so preoccupied by judging and condemning that we tear down our *own* homes with our own hands. The spirit of condemnation pervades the very being of the woman and erodes at the gentleness, peacefulness, and goodness her family deserves. She becomes a bitter woman and her life bears bitter fruit.[2]

When we approach parenting in this way, "holiness" is earned because we've successfully accomplished certain practices and tasks, not necessarily because we've fulfilled God's will. Never mind that we've abandoned charity and are unduly critical of the parents around us. Never mind that we've adopted practices that don't work for our children and our situation. None of that matters as long as we've checked the boxes, no matter what the personal cost to our family members or ourselves, and then aimed judgment against those who haven't yet made the grade.

I've been on the receiving end of judgment about the "right way" to parent as a Catholic, but I would be lying if I said I've never been guilty of scrutinizing other families who chose a path different than my own. I too have doled out unsolicited advice when it wasn't my place to do so. I can be as smug and critical as the next person, especially when I'm convicted about a certain approach. In these moments, though, it's helpful to remind myself that it's more important to me to behave lovingly to the parent standing in front of me rather than make sure the other parent knows I'm "right." I don't want to criticize or tear down the efforts of another mother just because they are different from my own. I don't want to sit in judgment of her; I want to support her, build her up, and assume she is doing the best she can given her circumstances.

In his apostolic letter *On the Dignity and Vocation of Women*, John Paul II explains that one of women's greatest gifts is sensitivity. This aspect of the feminine genius makes us able to perceive the inner life of another human being, to know the deepest needs of the human heart.[3] Because of our sensitivity, one thing all mothers should know is how hard it is to be a good mother and do our job well. Why, then, would we "make up litmus tests and then level judgments" against those who are trying really hard? Why would we decide whether another Catholic mom is living a good, holy life according to our standards?

A few years ago, my brother and I were having a conversation when I started to tell him what to do with his life. Ryan held up his hand to interrupt me and said, "Are you in my sandbox? Because you have plenty of sand in *yours*." I started laughing because I understood his point: I don't have to worry about managing

Ryan—I've got enough to worry about in my own life. The same is true when I'm tempted to concern myself with the parenting practices of my neighbors. I don't have time to check out their sand levels and the types of toys available in the box next to me because I've got a pretty full box to keep me busy. And the next time another parent attempts to offer me suggestions on the best way to conduct myself or my family, I can charitably redirect them back toward their own spots.

Keeping Our Eyes on Our Own Work

In John 21:21, right after Peter proclaims his love for Jesus three times and Jesus entrusts the Church once again into Peter's hands, Peter notices the beloved disciple John and asks, "'Lord, what about him?'"

Jesus says to Peter, "'What if I want him to remain until I come? What concern is it of yours? You follow me'" (Jn 21:22). "Follow me," Jesus tells Peter. "Don't worry about what I'm asking John to do. I have a different plan for him, and you don't need to know what that plan entails." The same is true for us; we must quit worrying about our neighbor's parenting plans and tend to the plan God has called us to, which is probably much different. Pride tempts us to wonder about what we see as the better, more prestigious path, but we must let those worries alone. Jesus wants us to pay attention to his call to us, and he wants us to be faithful and obedient to it and not to worry about his call to our neighbor. Jesus asked Peter to do one thing and John to do another. Both men had important tasks in the early Church, *both* men became saints, but the way they served was different.

There are many different paths to sanctity, and not one of them is necessarily "right" or "better" than the other. Dictators and despots are all the same: psychologically unbalanced with a proclivity for evil. When you consider the saints, on the other hand, they are all different—not one of them exactly like another except in their love and desire to do God's will. Evil is evil and looks the same; sanctity comes in thousands of shapes and sizes, in as many examples as there are saints in the history of the Catholic Church today.

Consider, for example, St. Rita, a devout woman who was pressured into marrying a quick-tempered, unfaithful, and abusive man. Throughout her eighteen-year marriage, Rita's husband verbally and physically abused her and was unfaithful. Rita's continuous patience and kindness inspired her abusive and demanding spouse to convert, but her husband was soon murdered thereafter because of a longstanding, unresolved feud. Left alone to raise her two boys, Rita attempted to encourage her sons toward peace, but they desired to avenge their father's death. Instead of losing her sons to mortal sin, Rita begged God to take her sons to heaven. A year later, St. Rita's boys were dead from dysentery.

Consider St. Elizabeth Ann Seton, a widow with five children; her dead husband's family rejected her after her conversion to Catholicism. She was penniless, with no husband and five kids, and she was probably feeling a tad desperate when she accepted a job offered to her to start a girls' school in another state.

Nothing about the lives or familial situations of Rita or Elizabeth was similar, and nothing about them resembled ease or perfection. If these women ever spent time comparing themselves to their neighbors, I'm convinced these saints would have had every reason to feel less than holy. It must have been humiliating for Rita, who originally desired to spend her days in quiet prayer as a nun, to have to endure the public spectacle caused by her pugnacious husband and sons. There is a unique and sad kind of loneliness Elizabeth must have experienced as a poor, widowed mother of five who had been abandoned by her family and friends.

These saints were in desperate situations. How often did they question their decisions and beat themselves up for their personal weaknesses? Perhaps they experienced moments of worry about what others thought of their situations.

St. Rita and St. Elizabeth probably would have preferred to choose certain parenting practices (such as active, involved Catholic husbands, for instance) over the realities they faced (a wayward, abusive spouse and a dead one), but instead they embraced and used their difficult obstacles as avenues to holiness. The saints didn't learn to love God and others so well in spite of the imperfection and challenges they faced. They learned to love God and others so well *because* of them. These women weren't born saints; Rita and Elizabeth *became* saints. They were refined in fire, a fire that burned the love for their own will right out of them and replaced it with a love for God's. Like these holy women, I'm called to sanctity not in spite of my familial and personal difficulties but *through* them.

Here is one truth we Catholic parents have to accept: we must quit worrying about what everyone else is doing and set to work becoming holy within the confines of our own particular families. St. Katharine Drexel once said, "It is a lesson we all need—to let alone the things that do not concern us. He has other ways for others to follow Him; all do not go by the same path. It is for each of us to learn the path by which He requires us to follow Him, and to follow Him in that path."[4] Another important truth is this: Just because we implement certain parenting practices does not mean our children will become practicing Catholics themselves. Life doesn't offer us those kinds of guarantees.

That mountain of perfect parenting practices you think are an insurance policy to raising Catholic kids? Surrender it. After reasonable discernment, pick a few practices, do your best, and then trust God to work out the details. That irreligious spouse who keeps you on your knees begging Jesus to convert him? That spouse and your prayers will make you a saint. That defiant, prodigal child who keeps you up at night with worry? She has been given to you for your holiness. Your mother-in-law, the one whose presence prompts you to utter (under your breath) every single curse word? One day you'll have to shine your halo in heaven because of her.

No family is perfect. (Even the one in the *Catholic Review* newspaper—the family who looks perfect, has multiple vocations, and a polished delivery—they sin too, I promise.) We all are shackled with our own personal weaknesses and the personal weaknesses of others, and these things make perfect family life impossible. We have a choice: we can waste time complaining about it, comparing our difficulties with those of others, and forcing solutions that don't work, or we can pull up our sleeves and devote ourselves to the work required of sanctity. My family isn't perfect and neither is yours, but they are perfect in the way God will use them to make us holy.

It's also important to remember that some families are confronted with much bigger issues than whether or not to continue breastfeeding, homeschooling, or co-sleeping. For instance, maybe one spouse has no faith in God while the other is committed to his or her faith. An atheist parent will certainly make evening Rosaries around a fire or Sunday Mass challenging. Maybe one spouse struggles with a severe addiction that inhibits intimate family life. A porn-reliant parent will circumvent developing authentic familial relationships. Maybe a couple might love the educational ideals of homeschooling, but the parent responsible for the children's education suffers from depression, burnout, or rage, making home education a nightmare for the parties involved. Many other couples face chronic issues such as alcoholism and drug use, joblessness, divorce, crippling anxiety and depression, and marital discord. Grave circumstances can keep conscientious parents from following through with ideal parenting practices.[5]

So let's have mercy on ourselves and let's have mercy on our fellow Catholic parents who aren't always able to institute the parenting practices they may desire. Unless we are failing in our moral obligations to raise Catholic children imbued with the faith, most of the parenting practices we choose reflect our *preferences*, not our religious and moral convictions. Let's assume we are all trying our very best to raise our kids to the best of our abilities, even if we're not able to attain the "ideal" as we've defined it. Let's have mercy on ourselves for the times when we have had to choose a less desirable approach than we originally intended, and let's have mercy on those parents who've had to do the same thing. And let's rally behind each other to offer love, support, and encouragement instead of our often unhelpful opinions. We can't ever fully know the situations or the reasons behind the decisions a family makes, but we can give each other love and the benefit of the doubt.

I've come a long way from the young parent I once was, obsessing about my inability to provide Gymboree classes for my kids or finding myself trapped on the phone while my daughter tossed beads on the floor. I have confidence now that my duties as a Catholic parent do not require Gymboree, but they do require me to love God and teach my children to do the same. My duties as a Catholic parent require me to bring my children to the sacraments, expose them to the teachings of the Catholic Church, and instruct them in spiritual and moral matters as best I can. The way I fulfill this obligation, however, will probably look different than the way you do it, but I guarantee all of our methods will be imperfect and messy and fraught with difficult moments.

And that's OK.

We're not required to be Catholic parenting all-stars, but we are required to be faithful to our job as Catholic parents, to stand back up after we fall flat on our Catholic parenting faces. Success isn't the goal of a Catholic parenting, but fidelity to God's call is.

If fidelity if good enough for God, it's good enough for me too.

The Best Parenting Practice I Know

A friend of mine came to visit last week with her small army of young children. We chatted while I slathered peanut butter and jelly on slices of wheat bread and threw them at the masses. Every five minutes, we filled requests for cups of water and changed diapers and broke up scuffles over toys. In between the commotion she asked, "How do you discipline your kids?"

I paused because her question, while excellent, was a rather weighty one I wasn't sure I was prepared to answer. I am *not* a parenting expert. I always joke God gave me all these kids because he knows how stupid I am: some people learn important parenting lessons after one or two children, but God knew it would take me six to get even the basics down! On top of being a slower learner, I tend to be a *reactor*, which is a nice way of saying I have a bad temper and sometimes yell.

And my children? While they are the most awesome people I know, they have their own set of idiosyncrasies that, when paired with my weaknesses, often lead to explosive results. My strategy for discipline is helter-skelter at best.

I fumbled around for a few minutes and tossed out a few ideas about how I deal with toddlers. None of the insights I shared were at all helpful, and the more I talked, the more idiotic I sounded. Fifteen years into this parenting gig and the only "tip" I had to offer is what I do when my toddler walks up and down my couch.

The tide of the conversation turned, though, when my friend confessed to me the guilt she experienced for the times she responded poorly to her children. As she spoke, I saw my much younger self in her struggles: I remembered feeling that earth-shattering love for all my little people, a love overshadowed only by my inability to parent them perfectly. I remembered my desire to raise my children in the Catholic faith and care for them as best I could but feeling a chronic frustration with my selfish, impatient, and reactive tendencies. I remembered the joy I experienced from being surrounded by my favorite people but also the crushing weight of responsibility I faced in raising them. I could identify with her feelings of failure and with her worry that she was warping her kids for all of eternity. That's when it dawned on me: I *do* have a discipline strategy, a method to help me when I want to be a better parent but am limited by my sin and humanity. I attend regular Confession.

After six children and fifteen years, the only strategy I've implemented that has effectively made me more patient and a more loving disciplinarian is confessing to a priest—*in persona Christi*—exactly how impatient and unloving I really am. The only thing that has helped me to respond instead of react to my children is to get on my knees and, in between sobs, relay to a priest that I sometimes behave worse than the toddler with whom I'm dealing. The only thing that has helped me get a handle on my temper is to say over and over "Bless me Father, for I have sinned again and again and again."

It is the frequent reception of the Sacrament of Penance that has supplied me with the gifts a parenting book, parenting practice, advice, or counseling hasn't: It's given me the ability to accept my sinful ways and trust God's love for me in spite of my weakness. It's given me the peace to parent these kids, even though I am so very broken. And it's given me the courage to "go, and sin no more."

The week before Good Friday this past spring, my six children and I waited over two hours for an open confessional. Standing in line was *hard*. By the end, the toddler was bolting down the aisle to get away from me and the four-year-old and six-year-old were quite loudly and quite openly declaring their boredom. All the kids were starting to lose it, and frankly, I was too.

But I stayed in line; I wouldn't have left if someone offered me a million dollars because I knew the importance of my silent witness. Without using any words, I was saying to my kids, "Children, your mother makes many mistakes. She is broken and imperfect. She sins many times over, but she knows where to go to ask for forgiveness, and she will crawl there to get it, if she must. She will wait for hours to see a priest, if that's what it takes to receive Christ's forgiveness. Children, your mother doesn't know everything, but she does know God loves her, and she knows he's waiting to offer her mercy. Your mother, children, knows where she can go for healing. And now because you've seen her go, you too will know where to find healing and mercy for all of your mistakes."

That's a discipline strategy worth implementing, I think.

Closing Prayer

Lord, sometimes I think I know better than you the right course of action for my family. My pride and my desire to control are so deep, Lord, that I don't take the time to discern your will before I insist on doing things my way. Help me to know what it is you desire for my own family and give me the courage to do those things well. Forgive me for persevering in an approach that wasn't what you wanted and for becoming distracted with my neighbor's work instead of maintaining a laser focus on my own.

Thank you for the painful growth you allowed me to experience when I was forced to take a different path than the one I might have chosen. I trust in your ability to bring tremendous good out of the less-than-perfect circumstances I sometimes face in family life, and I trust you will give me the grace to parent these children to the best of my abilities. Amen.

Discussion Questions

1. How do you handle children's extracurricular activities? Is your family life balanced or not?

2. Do you have a tendency to moralize certain parenting practices? Why or why not? What parenting practices do your friends make into moral issues? Why is the practice a moral issue, or why is it not?
3. Do you compare yourself against the activities and efforts of other parents? Are these comparisons generally helpful or unhelpful?
4. Have you ever had to abandon a "perfect" parenting practice in favor of a "lesser" one? Why? What did you learn?
5. Knowing that you can't force your kids to be or remain Catholic, how can you show them why the faith is so important?

CONCLUSION

Active love is labor and perseverance, and for some people, perhaps, a whole science. But I predict that even in that very moment when you see with horror that despite all your efforts, you not only have not come nearer your goal but seem to have gotten farther from it, at that very moment—I predict this to you—you will suddenly reach your goal and will clearly behold over you the wonder-working power of the Lord, who all the while has been loving you, and all the while has been mysteriously guiding you.

—Fyodor Dostoyevsky, *The Brothers Karamazov*

I laid my weary head against the confessional gate and sighed loudly, worn from the weight of my brokenness. We had waited a long time for an empty seat and an available priest. When it was my turn to enter, I knelt and recounted my sins—ones my heavenly Father already knew—and then I paused.

"I think," I rambled to the shadow lurking behind the screen, "I think I *am* getting better, Father, but I'm not getting better fast enough."

Silence settled within the dimly lit confines of the small booth as I waited for some direction and for some insight.

"Perhaps God isn't on your timeline for improvement," the priest responded.

I laughed out loud as the truth of this statement hit me upside the head like a foul ball outside of home plate. No one is on my timeline—not me, my husband, my kids, my extended family, or my friends, not even God.

"Hurry up, already," I instruct my kids throughout a day. They don't move fast enough, respond quickly enough to my suggestions for improvement. *When are they going to learn that their behavior simply isn't acceptable? How many times am I going to have to explain it to them, over and over like a broken record?* I wonder. When my daughter comes home, tears dripping down her face because the same kid has made the same rude comment for the third day in a row, I pray to muster words of compassion instead of irritation that she chose to ignore my advice to stay away from that kid.

"It won't happen again," one of my children often says in apology. I counter with, "How about you just tell me you're going to try harder?" because while we may want to eradicate a certain weakness from our very being, the fact is change is slow, hard, and time consuming. It requires work and grace and patience.

"There are just some things about myself I will never be able to fix," I told the same priest during a different meeting in the confessional.

"That may be true," he said, "The Serenity Prayer petitions God to help us accept the things we cannot change. You may not be able to eliminate some of the bad things about yourself, but it is possible for God to change you. That's where the sacraments and grace come in. He knows what you need, the minute you need it. It's important to come to him, to wait on him. It's important to *surrender*."

Surrender—that's a vastly different approach than the one I usually take, which includes strong-armed corrections of my faults as soon as possible. All my "self-improvement" plans have never been all that effective, really. If there's one thing I know it's that true change—true conversion—will only come when I'm able to pray and mean words like those found in the "Big Book" of AA: "Relieve me of the bondage of self, that I may better do Thy will."[1] True conversion will happen when I consistently wave the white flag, give myself up, and pronounce earnestly, "What is it *you* want, Lord?" C. S. Lewis once wrote,

> There must be a real giving up of the self. . . . As long as your own personality is what you are bothering about, you are not going to Him at all. The very first step is to try to forget about the self altogether. Your real, new self . . . will not come as long as you are looking for it. It will come when you are looking for Him. . . . The principle runs through all life from top to bottom. Give up yourself, and you will find your real self. Lose your life and you will save it. Submit to death, death of your ambitions and favorite wishes every day. . . . Keep back nothing. Nothing that you have not given away will be really yours. Nothing in you that has not died will ever be raised from the dead. Look for yourself, and you will find in the long run only hatred, loneliness, despair, rage, ruin, and decay. But look for Christ and you will find Him, and with Him everything else thrown in.[2]

I can stay cramped and insane, trying to impose my will onto all facets of life, or I can lose myself and find God. I can surrender to him and find freedom.

The Theology of the Donkey

I went to visit to my priest friend, Father, a few years ago to glean some direction from him in my prayer and personal life. Our discussion on my issues was cut short, however, when he asked, "Have I ever told you about the theology of the donkey?"

I shook my head no, wondering what the theology of the donkey had to do with my personal problems.

"I love the spirituality of the donkey," he said. "The donkey is very stubborn, you know. If you make the donkey mad, he'll kick and bray at you. But the donkey, when peaceable, can be very humble and hardworking. The donkey had a very important job in salvation history—the donkey was a throne for Mother Mary and baby Jesus."

I politely nodded. Father pointed to a statue of the Holy Family where Mary was prominently perched on a large, grey donkey.

"It's a beautiful statue, Father," I said.

"I noticed it in a hospital gift shop window one day as I was leaving. I just had to buy it because the donkey is the key component to the statue. See how he takes up most of it?"

I nodded my head again, noted the size of the rather large donkey carrying half of the Holy Family, and stifled a somewhat annoyed sigh.

What does a donkey have to do with anything? I wondered. *Why does he keep talking about donkeys?*

"In Spain in the 1930s there was a civil war, and all Catholic priests were being persecuted," Father continued again. "One day St. Josemaría Escrivá walked down the street when a man attacked him and started strangling him to death. Out of nowhere, another man came over, pulled the attacker off the saint, and threw the attacker to the ground. St. Josemaría Escrivá, lying on the cement and gasping for air, tried to thank the mysterious stranger.

"'That's for you, you mangy little donkey,' said the gruff stranger.

"The saint knew his guardian angel had saved him because the stranger called him 'mangy little donkey,' a title used by Escrivá to describe himself during prayer with God," Father finished.

"That's an amazing story," I said, and I meant it.

"Colleen, no matter how small we are, how small or insignificant, we can all bring Christ to the world, just like a mangy donkey."

"Huh," I said, ruminating about the role of the donkey in salvation history. It's a point I had never considered. I liked Father's explanation of the theology of the donkey and his story of St. Josemaría Escrivá, but I didn't think much more about it until the following evening.

My husband and I brought our children to a live nativity put on by the Franciscan friars at the Shrine of St. Anthony. After the nativity was over, I asked John to drive around the rather large property owned by the Franciscans because I wanted to see the beautiful buildings. It was dark out—past 9:00 p.m.—as we meandered down the long drive toward the shrine, which is when we noticed an enormous statue basking beneath a large spotlight. The marble glowed neon white against the sky's black backdrop.

"What is that?" John asked as he slowed the vehicle.

All of the kids and I leaned over to look.

"I've never seen a statue like that before in my life. Is that a donkey?" he asked.

We gazed at the larger-than-life image before us, a depiction of St. Anthony of Padua holding a large monstrance over his head with a donkey kneeling directly in front of him.

"I can't believe it," I exclaimed. "That's a donkey kneeling in front of St. Anthony! It's a donkey, John!"

My mind immediately went to the theology of the donkey and Father's story of St. Josemaría Escrivá. No one understood my excitement about a statue with a gigantic mule in it until I recounted Father's tale of St. Josemaría Escrivá as the mangy little donkey.

"That's the most awesome story I've ever heard," Patrick exclaimed when I finished. I winked in agreement.

"But that's not a statue of St. Josemaría Escrivá in it," John said. "That's St. Anthony. Why is a donkey kneeling before St. Anthony's monstrance?" he wondered.

I did a quick search on John's phone and within moments I relayed the famous story of St. Anthony and the kneeling donkey to everyone. The story tells of a man named Bonillo who openly declared to St. Anthony his disbelief in the true presence of Eucharist.[3]

"If the mule you ride adored the Body and Blood of Christ, would you believe then?" St. Anthony asked Bonillo during one of Bonillo's tirades against the Sacrament of the Eucharist.

"Even my mule wouldn't be stupid enough to kneel before a piece of bread," Bonillo responded, but St. Anthony pressed him again.

"Yes, but if the mule *did* adore Christ, would you believe?" St. Anthony asked.

Bonillo said if his donkey were to kneel before the Eucharist, he would believe. The two men agreed to a test. Bonillo would not feed the donkey for several days to make him good and hungry. Then Bonillo would present hay to the hungry donkey at the same time St. Anthony would expose the Blessed Sacrament, and they would see which the donkey would choose.

Bonillo spread the word. He wanted to make a fool of St. Anthony in front of the entire town and expose him as a fraud. On the day of the test, a large crowd gathered, and Bonillo led the donkey toward both the exposed Blessed Sacrament and a large pile of hay. The mule, though suffering from severe food depravation, walked over to the Blessed Sacrament and knelt in adoration. The crowd was amazed, and Bonillo was converted.[4]

I couldn't believe it.

In less than twenty-four hours, I had encountered not one but *two* famous saint stories about donkeys and had seen two separate statues depicting a donkey with Christ. I knew there was something here for me.

The Donkey and Me

How does the theology of the donkey apply to my life? I wondered as we drove the dark roads home.

I thought about the donkey stories for several days, and when I couldn't figure out what I was to learn, I took my quest to Google. I searched "characteristics of the donkey" and discovered a few important facts:

- a donkey makes decisions based on personal safety or best interest;
- a donkey possesses a loud bray which can last for up to twenty seconds and is a tool used to communicate with other donkeys; and
- a donkey bites, strikes with the front hooves, or kicks with the hind legs to defend itself.[5]

I also learned a donkey is a pack animal that, when properly trained, bears heavy loads—loads greater than stallions the same size can carry—for its master. Under the right conditions, the donkey is a dependable animal, hardworking and loyal. In order to be effective, however, the donkey has to first learn to trust its master to guide it in the right way. The donkey isn't any good at its job unless it is trained to listen.[6]

It appears the donkey and I had more in common than I originally thought. Stubborn? Highly developed sense of self-preservation? Loud? Bites and kicks in defense? I'm guilty of all this and more, and that's on a good day. Like a donkey, I need training to trust not in myself but in a loving master who guides me. This retraining makes me more dependent on my master, yes, but it makes me infinitely more effective than if I just swiped away at life on my own. The more I thought about it, the more I realized the donkey wasn't just some stupid, random animal Father wanted to discuss but an animal for me to emulate.

Zechariah 9:9 states, "Behold: your king is coming to you, a just savior is he, humble, and riding on a donkey, on a colt, the foal of a donkey." Jesus fulfills this Old Testament prophecy when he enters Jerusalem riding on that donkey Zechariah predicted. Upon first glance, it's strange Jesus would pick a donkey, isn't it? Wouldn't a fleet of chariots with powerful stallions be more appropriate for him? Fr. John Sullivan, O.C.D., explained to me recently that Jesus didn't just randomly hop on a donkey just because. Jesus carefully selected the donkey because the donkey was the exact type of animal royalty rode. The donkey symbolized to all of Jerusalem that Jesus truly was the King of kings, although not the warrior king they originally expected.

Jesus chose a humble, peaceable donkey, not a strapping mare, and that mule allowed Jesus to guide him and, in turn, aided in saving the world from sin. The donkey submitted to Christ and accomplished grand things in his name, and *this* is the lesson of the donkey for me, for all of us: Jesus wants us, the loud, braying, imperfect asses we are, to go where he calls us. He wants us to carry his load, to do the work of bringing others to him; and we can only complete this task, of course, if we abandon our "perfect" plans and the baggage that weighs us down. We must learn—just like that donkey did—to submit ourselves to him.

It's a noble task with eternal value.

I Will Fail, So I Must Pray

Learning to submit is a slow, humbling process though. It takes time and practice and effort—a lifetime of tweaking. Still today (and probably tomorrow) I fight my desire to do God's job. I must make a conscious effort to die daily to all my unhealthy tendencies and accept that God really does know better than I do (though I'm more than willing to offer feedback if he needs it). I have days when I worry and fret and reach out to grab the reins of control back.

But my good master doesn't release the reins.

He softly beckons me to a different path, one where he leads and I follow. My desire to control will never go away, but the repeated effort to turn my mind and heart to him—my master who is willing and waiting to help me—allows me to accept those things I can't control and gives me courage to change those things I can.

When I feel control creeping in, especially as it pertains to my family—there is a particular prayer I wrote to God, asking him to deliver me from my selfish, vain desires. I offer this prayer below because it might help parents just like me, struggling to let go and let God. Let's pray for each other and for our imperfect efforts to form our imperfect families.

May God bless and protect us all.

The Litany of Humility for Parents

O Jesus! Meek and humble of heart,

Hear me.

From the desire to have my children and myself be esteemed as intelligent and accomplished in the eyes of the world,

Deliver me, Jesus.

From the desire to have a picture-perfect Catholic family,

Deliver me, Jesus.

From the desire to have it appear as if my family and I have it all together,

Deliver me, Jesus.

From the desire to protect my children from all pain,

Deliver me, Jesus.

From the desire to have my family, especially my children, and me praised,

Deliver me, Jesus.

From the desire to have my family, especially my children, and me preferred to others,

Deliver me, Jesus.

From the tendency to compare my familial situation to another's,

Deliver me, Jesus.

From the desire to control my children's behavior and choices,

Deliver me, Jesus.

From the desire to be approved by other parents or by family members and even by my own children,

Deliver me, Jesus.

From the fear of being humiliated by wacky kid behavior or even by the sinful behavior of older children,

Deliver me, Jesus.

From the fear of warping my children and dooming them to failure because of screwy parenting,

Deliver me, Jesus.

From the fear of suffering rebukes from my grown children for the parenting decisions we made,

Deliver me, Jesus.

From the fear of being calumniated because we may make counter-cultural parenting decisions,

Deliver me, Jesus.

From the fear of being forgotten by my children when we have raised them and they leave,

Deliver me, Jesus.

From the fear of failing my children because of personal weaknesses and human inadequacies,

Deliver me, Jesus.

From the fear that my children will lose their faith in you and leave the Catholic Church,

Deliver me, Jesus.

From the fear that the world and all the evil in it will swallow my children whole,

Deliver me, Jesus.

From the fear that every other family is "functioning" and "normal" except for my own,

Deliver me, Jesus.

From the fear that taking care of myself mentally, spiritually, physically, and emotionally is selfish,

Deliver me, Jesus.

From the fear that my children must behave perfectly at Mass and know all the rote prayers and teachings of the Catholic Church or else we have failed in our catechetical duties,

Deliver me, Jesus.

From the fear that I have to make perfect parenting decisions
or else my children will be failures,

Deliver me Jesus.

That my children may love you above all things of this world,

Jesus, grant me the grace to desire it.

That my children may value the opinion of their future
spouses or superiors more than mine,

Jesus, grant me the grace to desire it.

That my children may one day chose their own vocational
responsibilities and set me aside,

Jesus, grant me the grace to desire it.

That my family may become holier than I am, provided that
I may become as holy as I should,

Jesus, grant me the grace to desire it.

Amen.[7]

NOTES

Foreword

1. Catherine de Hueck Doherty, *Poustinia: Encountering God in Silence, Solitude, and Prayer*, Madonna House Classics (Combermere, Ontario: Madonna House Publications, 2000), 62.

Introduction

1. See "Characteristics and Personalities of Adults Who Grew Up with Alcoholism in the Home," Searidge Foundation, last updated 2016, http://www.searidgealcoholrehab.com/article-adult-children-of-alcoholics.php.

Confession 1: I Don't Know How to Master Motherhood

1. Alcoholics Anonymous, *Twelve Steps and Twelve Traditions* (New York, NY: Alcoholics Anonymous World Services, INC, 2001), 5.

2. Jacques Philippe, *Interior Freedom* (New York: Scepter Publishing, 2007), 33.

3. Thérèse of Lisieux, *Story of a Soul: The Autobiography of Saint Thérèse of Lisieux*, 3rd ed., trans. John Clarke (Washington, DC: ICS Publications, 1996), 222–23.

4. See Heather King, *Shirt of Flame: A Year with Saint Thérèse of Lisieux* (Brewster, MA: Paraclete Press, 2011), 72.

5. Jean C. J. d'Elbee, *I Believe in Love: A Personal Retreat Based on the Writings of St. Thérèse of Lisieux* (Manchester, NH: Sophia Institute Press, 1974), 99.

Confession 2: I Don't Always Take Care of Myself As I Should

1. Josemaría Escrivá, *The Way* (New York: Scepter Press, 1982), 265.

2. See Robert Wicks, an interview by *US Catholic*, "Help Yourself: The Importance of Self-Care for Caregivers," *US Catholic*, April 2012, http://www.uscatholic.org/life/everyday-spirituality/2012/03 help-yourself-importance-self-care-caregivers.

3. Ignatius of Loyola, *Personal Writings*, (London: Penguin Books, 1996), 13.

4. James Martin, S.J., *The Jesuit Guide to (Almost) Everything: A Spirituality for Real Life* (New York: Harper Collins Publishers, 2012), 11.

5. Ibid., 187.

6. See ibid., 310–11.

7. See ibid., 358.

Confession 3: I Don't Know How to Keep My Kids Catholic

1. Sarah Mackenzie, *Teaching from Rest: A Homeschooler's Guide to Unshakeable Peace*, 2nd ed. (Camp Hill, PA: Classical Academic Press, 2015), 14.

2. Ibid., 15.

3. Jacques Philippe, *Interior Freedom*, 75.

4. See ibid.

5. Thomas Dubay, *Prayer Primer: Igniting a Fire Within* (San Francisco: Ignatius Press, 2002), 27–28.

Confession 4: I Don't Like Watching My Children Suffer

1. Simcha Fisher, "Here We Are," *National Catholic Register*, February 21, 2013, http://www.ncregister.com/blog/simcha-fisher/here-we-are.

2. Modified from Colleen Duggan, "The Cross of Motherhood: Watching and Waiting," CatholicMom January 10, 2010, http://catholicmom.com/2010/01/27/the-cross-of-motherhood-watching-and-waiting-by-colleen-duggan.

3. Modified from Colleen Duggan, "The Girl with the Silk," *Catholic Digest*, June 2011: 69.

4. Robert Helmfelt, Frank Minirth, and Paul Meier, *Love Is A Choice: Recovery for Codependent Relationships* (Nashville: Thomas Nelson Publishers, 1989), 79.

5. Duggan, "The Cross Of Motherhood."

6. Francis Xavier Nguyen Van Thuan, *The Road of Hope* (Boston: Pauline Books and Media, 2001), 211.

7. Ibid., 213.

8. Ibid., 208.

9. Leon Cristiani, *Saint Monica and Her Son Augustine* (Boston: Pauline Books and Media, 1977), 45–51.

10. Augustine, *Confessions* (Oxford: Oxford University Press, 2008), 49.

Confession 5: I Sometimes Compare Myself with Other Parents

1. Colleen Duggan, "Getting My Kids into Harvard Is Not My Endgame," Aleteia, May 31, 2016, https://aleteia.org/2016/05/31 getting-my-kids-into-harvard-is-not-my-endgame.

2. Elizabeth Foss, "Eating Our Own," *In the Heart of My Home* (blog), August 30, 2008, www.elizabethfoss.com/journal/reallearning/2008/08/eating-our-own.html.

3. John Paul II, *Mulieris Dignitatem: On The Dignity and Vocation of Women*, August 15, 1988, w2.vatican.va/content/john-paul-ii/en/apost_letters/1988/documents/hf_jp-ii_apl_19880815_mulieris-dignitatem.html.

4. Integrated Catholic Life, "Daily Quote from St. Katherine Drexel," August 24, 2010, www.integratedcatholiclife.org/2010/08/daily-quote-from-st-katherine-drexel.

5. Modified from Colleen Duggan, "We're In This Together: Struggles Every Catholic Parent Faces," Catholic Digest, June/July/August 2013: 16.

Conclusion

1. "Step 3: How It Works," accessed July 3, 2013, www.12step.org/the-12-steps/step-3.

2. C. S. Lewis, "The Real Self," in *A Year with C.S. Lewis: Daily Readings from His Classic Works*, ed. Patricia S. Klein (New York: HarperCollins, 2003), 219.

3. "Saint Anthony and The Real Presence," last updated September 2017, http://www.catholic-pages.com/mass/corpus.asp.

4. Ibid.

5. See Mike Thomas, "Donkey Facts," last updated 2016, www.mikesdonkeys.co.uk/facts.html.

6. See *Wikipedia*, s.v. "Donkey," last updated June 21, 2017, http://en.wikipedia.org/wiki/Donkey.

7. Modified from Rafael Merry del Val, "Litany of Humility," on EWTN's website, last modified 2016, www.ewtn.com/Devotionals/prayers/humility.htm.

Colleen Duggan is a Catholic writer whose work has appeared in *Catholic Digest, Creative Catechist, Catholic-Mom.com, Aleteia,* and *Integrated Catholic Life.* Duggan also is an art teacher and department head at a classical Christian academy in Maryland. She is a catechist, leads Bible studies, and speaks on Catholicism and Catholic parenting. She founded the women's ministry at her parish.

Duggan earned a bachelor's degree in religious studies and psychology from Saint Mary's College and a master's degree in education from the University of Notre Dame. She is a contributor to *The Catholic Mom's Prayer Companion.* She lives in the Harrisburg, Pennsylvania, area with her husband, John, and their children.

Lisa M. Hendey is Catholic blogger, speaker, creator of *CatholicMom.com,* and author of *The Handbook for Catholic Moms.*

CATHOLICMOM.com BOOKS

Ave Maria Press launched the CatholicMom.com Books series in 2012, building on the popularity of the award-winning *CatholicMom.com* website, as well as founder Lisa M. Hendey's books *The Handbook for Catholic Moms* and a *Book of Saints for Catholic Moms*. There are more than ten books in the series—written by trusted *CatholicMom.com* contributors and other Catholic authors—that address a variety of family and parenting issues from a thoroughly faith-filled perspective. Today, *CatholicMom.com* is a ministry of Holy Cross Family Ministries.

AVE
AVE MARIA PRESS

Look for these titles wherever books and eBooks are sold.
For more information, visit avemariapress.com.